D1234328

Black Soldiers
of New York State

Black Soldiers of New York State

A Proud Legacy

Anthony F. Gero

excelsior editions

State University of New York Press
Albany, New York

Published by the State University of New York Press, Albany

Cover image: postcard of African-American soldiers taken in New York City, ca. 1918–19, in the Anthony F. Gero collection; courtesy of Anthony F. Gero.

For information, contact State University of New York Press, Albany, NY
www.sunypress.edu

Production by Diane Ganeles
Marketing by Susan M. Petrie

Excelsior Editions is an imprint of State University of New York Press

Library of Congress Cataloging-in-Publication Data

Gero, Anthony F., 1949–
   Black soldiers of New York state : a proud legacy / Anthony F. Gero.
      p. cm.
   Includes bibliographical references and index.
   ISBN 978-1-4384-2615-0 (hardcover : alk. paper)
   ISBN 978-1-4384-2616-7 (pbk. : alk. paper)
   1. African American soldiers—New York (State)—History.   I. Title.

E185.93.N56G47 2009
355'.008996073—dc22   2008028299

10 9 8 7 6 5 4 3 2 1

#232786609

Contents

Illustrations

Preface

In *A Distant Mirror,* historian Barbara Tuchman quotes Voltaire, who said, "History never repeats itself, man always does." Such a case can be made when New Yorkers forget the role of their black citizens in the military from 1750 to 1950. Why has this happened so many times, when the documented records of these past events indicate the significant and proud role of New Yorkers of African descent? For example, in the eighteenth and early nineteenth centuries, black New Yorkers served, whether it was in the militia in the French and Indian War, or among the units raised for the American Revolutionary War, or in the ranks of New York's forces engaged in the War of 1812. Why, after each of these conflicts did succeeding generations forget, or were allowed to forget, the contributions of New York's black soldiers?

During the Civil War, the record of New Yorkers in the 54th Massachusetts Volunteer Infantry and the 20th, 26th, and 31st United States Colored Troops, along with the intrepid Harriet Tubman who served as military scout and nurse, proved their gallantry. As Colonel Thomas Wentworth Higginson of the 33rd Regiment, U.S.C.T. said: "Till the blacks were armed, there was no guaranty of their freedom. It was their demeanor under arms that shamed the nation into recognizing them as men."[1] In 1863 the famous abolitionist, Frederick Douglass, who lived and wrote in Rochester, New York, expressed his views on black New Yorkers then joining the 54th Massachusetts Volunteer Infantry. At recruitment centers in Buffalo, Rochester, Oswego, Syracuse, Auburn, Elmira, and other sites in New York, volunteers enlisted for the Civil War. With their enrollment came hope, for as Douglass said, "Let the black man get upon his person the brass letters U.S.; let him get an eagle on his buttons and a musket on his shoulder, and bullets in his pocket, and there is no power on earth which can deny that he has earned the right to citizenship."[2]

After this tragic war, had not the official records shown that black New Yorkers helped save the Union? Why had their demeanor under arms been forgotten after the war in New York State? Additionally, why was a colored line maintained in the Empire State's military forces from the end of that war until World War I that excluded New Yorkers of African heritage? In New York State's National Guard, from 1866 to 1915, no unit of black New Yorkers was allowed to join. Other states, including Connecticut, Rhode Island, Massachusetts, Pennsylvania, Ohio, Illinois, and even Virginia, Georgia, and North Carolina, had segregated black National Guard units, but in the Empire State, efforts failed to see even a segregated company, battalion, or regiment enrolled between 1866 and 1897. Why? New York authorities did not even authorize a black volunteer unit for the Spanish-American War in 1898. Other states, several among those just mentioned did, but why had New York State failed to do so?

When the twentieth century arrived, as Winston Churchill said, with its "blood red dawn," a great war in Europe threatened America. Black New Yorkers were prepared to take up arms in defense of their nation, but why did they have to prove their worth again to join? Only in 1916, through the efforts of prominent black and white individuals, did New York State finally sanction the 15th Regiment of New York's National Guard. When the federal government created the American Expeditionary Force (AEF), the 15th Regiment, which had been federalized, was redesignated as the 369th United States Infantry and was assigned to an African-American division, the 93rd. When the 92nd Division was also established as an African-American formation, the 367th Infantry was allocated in the division's table of organization. In the 367th ranks were many black New Yorkers. The combat records of the 367th and 369th were honorable, which was remarkable since, in many cases, these soldiers faced two enemies: the enemy overseas and racism in the AEF and at home, in New York.

Once these black veterans came back to the States, their service record was downplayed and revised to fit patterns of segregation, so very prevalent in the 1920s and 1930s. Despite the African-American community's high hopes of gaining equality through supporting the war effort, a racial backlash took hold. Although the 369th Regiment was retained in the state's National Guard and black New Yorkers were allowed to soldier on, such activities occurred only in the New York City area. Other regions, which could have supported black National Guard organizations, saw none formed and a new color line was maintained in the Empire State's National Guard. When World War II finally burst upon America in December 1941 black New Yorkers went into the federal armed forces. Since the evil of fascism cut across all social strata in New York State, New York's black sons and daughters answered the call to duty. As they went off to Europe or the Pacific, the New York Guard (NYG), a home defense force, was reconstituted in 1940. In that force, by 1942 a segregated 15th Regiment, NYG was raised in the New York City area. Why were NYG units of African-Americans not raised in Buffalo, or Rochester, or Syracuse as well?

A hint of what happened in New York State's military forces from 1750 to 1950 can be found in Richard Dalfiume's *Desegregation of the United States Armed Forces* (1969). The author writes on page 1, "Throughout American history the black American viewed his military service in the nation's conflicts as proof of his loyalty and as a brief for his claim to full citizenship. White Americans appear to have realized this, and they continually sought to restrict or downgrade the black soldier's military service." From the evidence in New York State's history, this national trend was also the pattern in New York for more than two hundred years.

Yet, as Tobias Smollet said, "Facts are stubborn things," and the facts prove the major contributions of black New Yorkers as soldiers from 1750 to 1950. As a single-volume history, *Black Soldiers of New York State* will set forth those facts, creating a view that is compelling in its scope and breadth. However, *Black Soldiers of New York State* is not meant to be a final study, as many researchers continue to find new evidence about the service of New York's black soldiers before 1950, which may not appear in this present volume. As for any errors in this book, I will take responsibility for them and beg the reader's leniency. I hope that if any have made it through, they are small in nature.

As English essayist Joseph Addison wrote, "What sculpture is to a block of marble, education is to the soul." The purpose of *Black Soldiers of New York State* is to educate and from that, each can judge whether the second half of Addison's statement is true.

Acknowledgments

Published histories are not researched without help; therefore, I wish to gratefully acknowledge those, past and present, who have assisted in my explorations: Colonel John R. Elting (USA-Ret.); Colonel Edward Milligan (USA-Ret.); Captain Fitzhugh McMaster (USN-Ret.); René Chartrand; Wayne Colwell; Al Haarmann; C. R. Gibbs; Philip G. Maples; Dale Post; Robyn Warn; Jim Morphet; Ernie Harris; Orton Begner; Rick Ugino (New York Guard); Brian L. Dunnigan; Fred Gaede; David Sullivan; Dale Beiver; Marko Zlatich; Roger Cunningham; Gerald Kennedy; Tom Rodgers; Joe LoPiccolo; Alan Ferguson, Kaitlyn Greenidge; Wallace F. Workmaster; Paul Dasans; Sheila Tucker, Cayuga County Historian; Eileen McHugh, director of the Cayuga Museum; Professor Louis Gebhard (S.U.C. at Cortland), and Dr. Michael Rinella, Susan M. Petrie, Diane Ganeles, and Pat Hadley-Miller at State University of New York Press.

Special thanks also go to Professor Judith Wellman (S.U.C. at Oswego); Mrs. Mary Gilmore of the history room at Seymour Library; Steve Erskine, former head librarian at Seymour Library (Auburn) and the interlibrary loan staff of that fine institution; William Gladstone whose personal knowledge of the United States Colored Troops was invaluable; and finally Laura Larson and John Patterson whose advice and editing skills were very constructive.

Military artists and researchers Alan Archambault, Raymond Johnson, Barry E. Thompson, H.C. McBarron, Loy Conley, Ron Spicer, Pete Copeland, Dave Abbott, Richard Warren, and Tom Jones of the Company of Military Historians helped to visualize, through their artworks, the individual as a soldier and not as a mannequin.

Fellow researchers and artists Roger Sturcke and Eric Manders have been, over the decades, of tremendous assistance as laborers in the field of military history, good friends, and muses in life.

For my wife, Linda Crye-Gero, whose love of genealogy, life, and cats has been a benchmark in my life, along with my daughters Theresa and Katherine, go sighs of love too deep for words.

Finally to my mother, Lillian (Cutro) Gero and my father, Samuel (Grigolio) Gero who were a part of that "greatest generation" and who, from my birth in April of 1949, raised me with patience and wisdom, I offer a humble thank you.

Chapter 1

The Missing Pages, 1750 to 1815

In 1919 Laura E. Wilkes, a teacher in the public schools of Washington, DC, wrote *Missing Pages in American History: Revealing The Services Of Negroes In The Early Wars In The United States Of America, 1641–1815.*[1] In her foreword, Wilkes states:

> A patient research, extending over a period of six years, has given the author the courage to send out this volume. It has also convinced her that the Negroes of America have done their bit in every war and taken no small part in every military movement made for the salvation of this country from the time of the earliest settlement. The facts found herein are taken from colonial records, state papers, assembly journals, histories of slavery, and old time histories of various colonies, and of the republic. The reader can easily verify this statement by using the bibliography at the end of the work.
>
> While it is impossible to gather all of the truths concerning this matter, it is doubtless true, that much more, than is here chronicled, will be available to the student of this particular department of history, if he shall have leisure and funds to dig deeper into half-forgotten traditions of old towns and villages. That these pages may prove a stimulant for further research, by others, their

writer ardently desires and she earnestly hopes the book will eventually be read collaterally, with the histories of the United States,
by every one who can be inspired by its information.

What an inspiration Wilkes' book could have been, but sadly
for the general public, the work was mainly forgotten, except to
inquisitive historians and scholars. Her call for African-American
soldiers to be "collaterally" included among the general histories of
the United States did not happen, as events after 1919 proved.

In that flow of history before World War I, I have decided
to begin *Black Soldiers of New York State* at an arbitrary point, in
the mid-eighteenth century with the French and Indian War.[2] As
Wilkes indicated, records reveal that the New York militia was
integrated. Upon my foray into the New York Provincial Muster
Rolls, the designations "Free Negro," "Negro," or "Mulatto" appears by some names.[3] For the years 1758, 1760, 1761, and 1762,
the lists show such men on the rolls.[4] For instance, in 1758 the
militia of Queens County, West Chester County, Orange County,
and Suffolk County have men labeled as "Free Negro," or "Negro" or "Mulatto" in various companies. As an example, Scudder
Samson, "a free Negro," of Suffolk County, was listed on the
rolls for 18 April, 1758, while in West Chester County in that
year, "Jeffery Garret...b Westchester...Labourer, Capt. Israel
Underhill...Negro" was registered.[5]

Although the total of Free Negroes, Negroes, and Mulattos
for the entire New York provincial militia was approximately
eleven to fourteen men for each year between 1758 and 1762, some
individuals' names appeared more than once. For example, a man
designated as "Kellis, Molato (sic): Age 18, b Suffolk, Lab.," from
a Captain Strong's company of Suffolk County is listed as having
passed muster in April 1759 and again in April 1760.[6] Whether he
was a free man is open to debate, but even though the total number
of men of African descent is not sizable for the entire militia, New
York's provincial force was integrated between 1758 and 1762.

A reconstruction of an African-American militiaman, Colonial New York, circa 1755 to 1760 by Eric Manders. *(Original sketch in the Anthony Gero Collection)*

There are indications that the "New York Battalions" or, as they were sometimes referred to in contemporary eighteenth-century accounts, "Regiments," which numbered one through three, may have had scattered African-Americans in them. Raised between 1758 and 1762, and uniformed in 1758 in plain green coats, these battalions were a vital part of the colony's forces.[7] Other provinces, like South Carolina, North Carolina, Virginia, New Jersey, Connecticut, and Massachusetts, used freedmen and slaves in their militia between 1755 and 1762.[8] Due to manpower needs, even the French and Spanish employed Free Negroes and mulattos in their colonial forces.[9] As a result, New York, in a hesitant and small way, was following an accepted military practice in North America, but this does not mean that large-scale integration was generally accepted during these colonial times.

Wilkes states, "Black militiamen were seen also at this period at Fort Williams, a stockade on the road to Oswego, New York. This place was at the southwestern end of Lake George and was built in 1735."[10] Whether these black militiamen were from New York or neighboring colonies is unclear as research continues on them.

African-Americans appear to have served in the British Army in North America, but the question is in what capacity and in what numbers.[11] There are hints that Roger's Rangers, a famous colonial unit, may have had an African-American or two in their various companies.[12]

Researchers will undoubtedly over the next decades discover even more information on African-American soldiers. Furthermore, in the colonial and Revolutionary War naval services and merchant marine from 1755 through 1783, black sailors served onboard ships. Since their role is outside the scope of this book, the reader can consult other sources on black sailors.[13]

Documents indicate that, although small in total numbers, colonial New York had elements of an integrated militia system during the French and Indian War. When one considers the global empire building that the European powers were engaged in from 1750 to the end of 1764, the participation of black soldiers in the Americas should be noted not as a matter of political correctness, but as historical fact.

As the rewards of victory can often spell future disaster, British authorities made decisions and policies in the late 1760s and early 1770s, which helped fan the rebellious nature of colonial Americans. By 1775, war with Great Britain had become unavoidable. Sides had been chosen; and, as result of subsequent events in and around Boston, and with the issuance of the Declaration of Independence in 1776, the colonies had erupted in armed rebellion. The separation of Britain's thirteen colonies could only be accomplished or resisted, after that, by force of arms. In those turbulent years, African-Americans began to determine how they felt about colonial independence and personal freedom. Their record of service to the Patriot cause across the thirteen colonies, or among the British forces and its hired auxiliaries sent to America, have been revealed in great detail by eminent historians, such as John Hope Franklin, Benjamin Quarles, and others.[14] Since my book is focused on New York's part in events from 1764 through 1815, what is presented next relates primarily to New York's soldiers of African descent.

Between 1764 and 1775, much is yet to be discovered on the role of black New Yorkers. One could assume that its colonial militia may have contained scattered individuals, but speculative history can be grounds for much misinformation. Other provinces, such as New Hampshire in its 11th Regiment of Provincial Militia in 1774 to 1775, had freed men serving, but did New York do the same in its provincial militia?[15] A hint of what might have happened in New York between 1764 and 1775 is contained in Quarles' work, "In New York the militia act of April 1, 1775, it stipulated that 'all bought servants during their Servitude shall be free from being listed in any Troop or Company within this Colony.' "[16] As this legislative act suggests, from 1764 to 1775, resistance to black involvement as slaves had grown, and the exclusion of all but Free Negroes from the militia was now the standard for New York.

With New York City being the object of British retaliatory plans for the summer of 1776, the necessity of raising large numbers of men for the Continental cause took hold. Congress ordered that, on January 16, 1776, the restriction for Free Negroes reenlisting be lifted.[17] In New York, and all across New England, the Middle Colonies, and the South, provincial legislatures tried to raise men, often despite racial barriers.[18] Wilkes found that in New York: "The name of 'Negro Tom' appears as early as March 18, 1776, on the rolls of the Orangetown, New York, regiment, as a drummer in the company of Capt. Egbert. Philip Field is mentioned as having

A water color drawing of a black soldier in the Rhode Island Light Infantry Company, ca. 1780–1781 by Barry E. Thompson. *(Anthony Gero Collection)*

enlisted April 15, 1777, in the Second New York Regiment. This man was a slave of Duchess County, New York. He died in Valley Forge, August, 1778."[19]

Historian Benjamin Quarles found evidence that a slave owner named David Belknap, summoned to Fort Montgomery, in New York sent his slave who, after "faithfully performing his duty, died while being held a prisoner by the British."[20] Perhaps Philip Field had also been sent by his owner while the drummer "Negro Tom" might have been brought to this company of the 2nd Militia Regiment as a slave, a practice not uncommon in colonial units. Some slaves in New York, like Peter Williams Sr., defied their Loyalist masters and decided to support the revolution.[21]

The Provincial Congress, under the direction of its president, John Hancock, called for large-scale military works to be created to defend New York City. These fortifications were, in part, dug by Negroes from the New York City area. These men were drafted from their masters who lived in the city and surrounding areas and were put to work on the defenses. With pick-axe and hoes, these slaves were assigned to build the fortifications to try and hold off the British juggernaut headed for this vital colonial city.[22]

By 1779 Wilkes states that General Anthony Wayne used a local man "Pompey Lamb, a Negro on a nearby farm," as a spy to help scout the British defenses at Stony Point, which Wayne planned to

A water color drawing of a black soldier in Butler's Rangers, a Loyalist unit, ca. 1777 by Barry E. Thompson. (*Anthony Gero Collection*)

attack. The assault, successfully carried out in July of that year, was one of the great American victories of the war. Among the prisoners taken by Wayne's men were several Negroes in British employ.[23]

On March 20, 1781, the legislature of New York passed an act that allowed masters to enlist their slaves for the Continental cause. If the slave served for three years, they would be freed, something that was being done in other colonies as well. The act also called for the raising of two regiments of black soldiers for New York's frontier defense.[24] Whether these separate black regiments were actually recruited and raised in New York State is still being researched.[25]

In the January 1783 campaign ordered by General Washington against the British garrison at Oswego, among the forces that Colonel Marinus Willet of New York took was the Rhode Island Regiment. This unit had a long and proud combat history with the Continental Army and was made up of black enlisted men with white officers. An African-American New Yorker named Henry Bakeman, who enlisted at Stone Arabia, Montgomery County in 1781, reportedly accompanied Willet's campaign to Oswego, which resulted in Bakeman's crippling, due to the extreme exposure endured on the march.[26]

The French and Spanish allied with the Continental cause had black soldiers among the troops they sent to fight. Many sources indicate that units of the British Army, as well among its Loyalist troops, and Germanic units hired to serve in America, had black men as soldiers.[27] For example, Butler's Rangers, a Loyalist unit formed by Tories in upstate New York, several black men did their duty as soldiers. The Black Pioneers, raised from men of African descent in the New York City area served, too. Following the Treaty of Paris in 1783, many of these men went to Canada and are listed in the famous source *The Book of Negroes*.[28]

With the evacuation of New York City on November 25, 1783, the accomplishments of New York's black soldiers in the creation of the American nation was a fact. Some records indicate that in the land bounty rights given to veterans to settle in the upstate New York from 1781 to 1794, several black New Yorkers were listed. Their names are filed under the heading of "Assignors" and read, "Jack(Negro) . . . Murray Jack(Negro) . . ."[29] Regrettably, no other men in this 1901 source bear this designation, but what this roll shows is that, as veterans, these two men were assigned their land bounty by a grateful New York State government. From 1783 through 1811, what took place in New York's militia with regard to its black men as freemen or slave? In other states of the young republic, the debates on slavery, the status of freedmen, and their role in the militia was wide-ranging.[30] At the national level, there are indications of black sailors serving during the Quasi-War with France, but whether they were in the fledgling American army is being researched.[31]

In the Empire State the legacy of its black soldiers during the Revolutionary War was allowed to wither on the vine, while their status in the militia, if any, is unclear.[32] Some states, like Georgia, still had slaves enrolled in scattered militia companies, while others, like Virginia, South Carolina, Pennsylvania, and New Jersey restricted the enlistment of freedmen to musicians or labor troops.[33] In the active militia forces of the New York State, the number of free black men, mulattos, or even slaves enrolled for militia duty seems to have been meager, between 1783 and 1811.

From 1803 to 1811, international tensions, precipitated by the Napoleonic Wars, were felt in New York State. Prior to 1812 the Empire State held a key position in the geography of America. With its important harbor at New York City and, in the north and west of the state, along its extensive border with British Canada, New York would be a major theater of military operations if war with Great Britain came. Once war was declared in the spring of 1812, political elements in New York State and among its militia forces supported the conflict.

During these years a question arose: what would be the role of black New Yorkers if war came? In the New York City area there were enough freemen and slaves in the total population of the city to help support the war, but would black New Yorkers be allowed to serve, and in what numbers, and in what capacity? An interesting item on an attempt to raise units from New York City's African-American population appears in 1812, when Governor Daniel Tompkins replied to a request, sent to his office, proposing to raise "men of color" for the war. The reply from the governor's office states:

....
...................Adjutant Generals Office
....
...................Albany, 20 July 1812
To Mr. R. Stevens
Sir
If you contemplate raising men of color for the United States army, your application for that purpose must be made to the President; if however, it is your desire to have a corps of them organized for the service of this State, it cannot be done, because the Comm'r in Chief has no authority to do so.
Your Ob't Servant
Ulm Paulding, Jun, Adj Genl.[34]

As commander in chief of the New York Militia, the governor felt he had no authority to raise such a corps in his state. Since no further mention of such a corps is found in Tompkins Papers until October 1814 one can assume no unit was raised in 1812 or 1813. Just who this "Mr. R. Stevens" is remains unclear.

However, from actions of the New York State Legislature in early fall of 1814, the matter had not ended. On October 24 the New York Legislature directed to be raised, "by voluntary enlistment, two regiments of free men of color for the defense of the state for three years, unless sooner discharged...." The strength of these two regiments was to be "one thousand and eight able-bodied men, . . ." while the commissioned officers "shall be white men." This order also allowed slaves to be enlisted if their masters granted permission and were appropriately compensated; but were these regiments ever really recruited and put into the field?[35]

In that regard, the contemporary records are somewhat tantalizing. Based on a reported Congressman Martingale's account, delivered before the United States Congress in January 1828, he stated: "Slaves or negroes who had been slaves were enlisted as soldiers in the war of the Revolution: and I myself saw a battalion of them,- as fine a martial looking men as I ever saw attached to the Northern army in the last war,- on its march from Plattsburg to Sacket's(sic) Harbor, where they did service for the country with credit to New York and honor to themselves."[36] If Martingale is to be believed, a battalion of these men was sent up to Sackett's Harbor, but countering his statement are a series of letters Governor Tompkins sent to the United States Secretary of War, James Monroe, on November 5 and 6, 1814, and on December 12, 1814. In these letters, Tompkins conveys the strong belief that these regiments would receive state bounties and would replace an equal amount of New York State militia, then in service, but he wanted assurances from the national government that these men of color would be clothed and subsisted by the federal government. It also appears, from the phrasing in Tompkins' letters, that these black men would stay in the New York City defenses, along with the newly authorized Sea Fencibles companies who were recruited among sailors in the city and were raised to help man the fortifications that formed New York City's defenses.[37]

With the war ending in January 1815, however, these black New York troops were short-lived, and as a result major histories on the War of 1812 have little on their actual service.[38] No data on these black soldiers having been at Sackett's Harbor in late 1814, other than Congressman Martingale's account, has yet been found.[39] There the matter rested, until a new item on black New

Yorkers in the War of 1812 was published. In the *New York Herald* of August 24, 1814, this local notice appeared:

> Patriotism of the Africans. This morning between 800 and 1000 of the hardy and patriotic sons of Africa, accompanied by a delightful band of music and appropriate flags, crossed the ferry at Catharine slip, to work on the fortifications at Brooklyn heights. These men, knowing the value of freedom, are anxious to defend it, and too much praise cannot be bestowed on them for their voluntary exertion.[40]

What this contemporary account shows is the voluntary organization of between eight hundred and a thousand African-Americans, in what I will call a "labor battalion." Since their formation predates the October 24, 1814, authorization of the New York State Legislature, which directed "two regiments of free men of color" to be raised, could the August activities of New York City's sons of African descent have prompted the October legislation? I believe it did.

New York City's black population seems to be volunteering in much the same way as had Philadelphia's. When asked for aid by the Philadelphia Vigilance Committee in 1814, Absolem Jones, Richard Allen, and James Forten, all leading black citizens of the city, helped secure voluntary service of black Philadelphians in erecting defenses for the city.[41] However, without actual names of any of these black New Yorkers who served, in either August or October, a nagging doubt continues: were some of them sent up to Sackett's Harbor?[42] The numbers of New York City's black residents who wished to serve in 1814 was substantial, as seen by the 1814 newspaper article and probably explains why the New York State Legislature in October 1814 authorized two regiments of black New Yorkers for the northern border's defense.

What of the United States Army units then on duty in New York State? Did they have freemen, mulattos, or slaves serving here?

If the answer is yes, were any of these men from New York State? Evidence on black soldiers in the 1812–1815 period for the Regular Army, outside New York, is growing. For two examples, in the 7th Regiment, United States Infantry, Jordan B. Noble, "a young mulatto drummer," served with the regiment at New Orleans from 1813 through 1815, while in the 38th U.S. Infantry, at Fort McHenry in 1814, William Williams, a mulatto, was on the muster rolls.[43] As researchers continue to uncover data, more men of color will appear as having served in the United States Army from 1812 through 1815. Did similar enlistments happen in New York State?

In the case of the famous 13th Regiment, United States Infantry, recruited primarily in New York State, and which served gallantly from the Niagara frontier to Sackett's Harbor, as of yet no evidence has surfaced on Negroes or mulattos in its ranks.[44] Robert E. Greene's research on the 25th Regiment of Infantry, which fought on the Niagara frontier and garrisoned Sackett's Harbor, shows that a soldier named Jacob Dexter, described as a colored man, may have been on its muster lists from 1814 to 1815.[45]

As a last example, the payroll of a company of artificers, under Ira Floyd, assistant superintendent, stationed at Burlington, Vermont, and who may have been at the battle of Plattsburgh in 1814, lists thirteen black men on its payroll.[46] Whether these African-Americans were from New York State cannot be confirmed from this company's payroll, but their names and designations are there.

On United States ships of the "fresh water navy," employed on the Great Lakes or Lake Champlain during the war, there is strong evidence of black sailors.[47] From the main American naval base at Sackett's Harbor to the port at Oswego, from the Niagara frontier or along Lake Erie, and finally at the naval engagement at Plattsburg, black sailors fought and died. Just how many of these men were from New York is still being researched. The probability is high for their service since New York City was a major port, with many black sailors ready to serve. For example, in the case of some privateers

A water color of a Freed Black seaman in the United States Navy, ca. 1812–1814 by Barry E. Thompson. *(Anthony Gero Collection)*

like the *Governor Tompkins*, sailing under authorization of New York State, black men were aboard while at the naval engagement on Lake Erie in 1813, Anthony Williams, "a colored man . . . served on the *Somers*, one of Commodore Perry's vessels . . ."[48]

The British and Canadian forces had black men in the ranks during the war. Some of these black Canadians traced their ancestors to black Loyalists who had settled in Canada, while others were more recent freedom seekers. Whether it was at the famous battle at Queenston Heights in 1812, with Captain Robert Runchey's company of black men, or as small part of the Canadian Voltigeurs, black men did their duty. In the British fresh waterfleets on Lake Erie, Ontario, and Champlain, and along the Atlantic coast, the Royal Navy and the Royal Marines, had men of color in service.[49]

During the campaign at New Orleans in December 1814 and early January 1815, the American battalion of "Free Men of Color" fought bravely, especially when General Andrew Jackson ordered a night attack on the British camp to try and confound the British as to his strength. When the grand assault of the British finally fell on Jackson's lines on January 8, 1815, helping to hold a part of the American front stood the 7th United States Infantry, along with its mulatto drummer, Jordan Noble.[50] As a result of Jackson's successful defense of this city, the American victory passed into legend and catapulted Jackson to the status of hero, then president. Ironically, among the British troops brought to take this vital port city was one of the West India Regiments, the 5th. These West India Regiments, numbered 1 through 6, were made up of black men whose origins, in part, can be traced to ex-slaves who fled with the British evacuation of the thirteen former colonies in 1783 and who had settled in the West Indies.[51]

The evidence is clear that men of African descent served on both sides in the War of 1812, and in some of the most important land battles and naval engagements. The armed forces of the United States and various state militias, including New York State, had black soldiers and sailors in them. Why then, after 1815, was their record largely forgotten, downplayed, or revised?

Conclusion

The facts of history should not be changed, despite revisionist historians' efforts to do so. Wilkes sought to rectify such omissions in 1919 and *Black Soldiers of New York State* attempts to do so today. After the War of 1812 ended, African-American involvement in the Empire State's militia faded and from 1816 to 1850; they were largely excluded from her militia. However, when the events of the 1850s and early 1860s became so tragic as to evolve into secession, white and black New Yorkers stood ready to defend the Union and to destroy America's institutionalized slavery.

Chapter 2

The Great Omission
and the Civil War,
1816–1866

From 1816 to the 1850s, African-Americans serving in the New York State Militia (NYSM) were involved in the great omission. Based on documentation uncovered to date, there is a huge gap of evidence concerning their possible service. Although it seems probable that after the gradual end of slavery in New York State through the efforts of the New York Manumission Society by 1827, freemen of African descent might have served in the NYSM, where is the confirmation to prove this?[1]

After the War of 1812, the militia organization of New York's enrolled or common militia became one of political patronage and, by the late 1830s, had degenerated into buffoonery. As a result of widespread antimilitia protests in the 1840s, the entire system was forced to change so that the traditional enrolled militia system, encompassing all able-bodied men, became a volunteer system of citizen-soldiers. These men formed either companies or regiments of like-minded individuals who wanted a military experience. They usually uniformed and armed themselves with official sanction by the Adjutant General's office of the state.[2]

United States Army regulations in 1820 and 1821 restricted enlistment to only "free white males." In the navy, by 1839, enlistment of black sailors had grown so disproportionately to that of white sailors that, under pressure of southerners opposed to such integration, the Secretary of the Navy tried to limit black sailors to 5 percent of total naval personnel.[3] During the Second Seminole War of 1838 to 1842, black men became involved. In the fighting in Florida, records indicate that Negroes took part on both sides.[4]

In Pennsylvania, some militia units, like the State Fencibles of Philadelphia, hired the famous Frank Johnson's Colored Band to provide martial music during the 1820s.[5] In some southern states, slaves could be enlisted in militia units. For example, the elite Republican Blues, 1st Regiment, Georgia Volunteers, from 1859 through 1860, had black drummers who paraded with the regiment when it visited New York City in 1860.[6] Other states may even have had freemen in their militias, more probably in the Northeast, such as Massachusetts, but research continues to find documentation on their service, if any, during the years before the Civil War.[7]

Just where did black New Yorkers fit into the NYSM between 1816 and 1850? From 1816 to 1850, evidence of their service, if any, is meager. From New York State records concerning those who were eligible for militia service in 1832, 1846, and 1847, it seems New York was following the Federal Militia Act of 1792, which said that "All able bodied white male citizens, between ages of eighteen and forty-five" would be enrolled and liable for service in the militia.[8]

By the early 1850s national events on slavery's extension into the territories, the Fugitive Slave Act and the actions of abolitionists had made a major impact on various states including New York. As a result, some evidence indicates that by the mid-1850s, black citizens in the New York City area were attempting to form military companies that may have tried to join the NYSM. For example, through the efforts of William C. Nell's research, one can catch a contemporary glimpse of what was happening in New York City. In 1855, Nell wrote:

> Within a recent period, several military companies have been formed in New York City, exclusively of colored men. They have been organized, in part, through the exertions of Captains Simmons and Hawkins, and are designated as the 'Hannibal Guards,' the 'Free Soil Guards,' and the 'Attucks Guards.' The New York Tribune says of one of these companies, in announcing their parade, that 'They looked like men, handled their arms like men, and should occasion demand, we presume would fight like men.' . . .[9]

Nell's contemporary account is significant because it names the three companies forming in New York City and provides us with two men who might have been officers in one of these companies or who may have helped form them. Whether Captains Simmons and Hawkins were African-Americans or white men, because no first names were given in Nell's work, makes documenting their status difficult. Some white officers, like Colonel John Cochrane of the 65th New York Volunteers, a nephew of the famous abolitionist Gerrit Smith, did call for the recruitment of black soldiers in November 1861. In 1864 another famous New Yorker, General Daniel Sickles, lent his support to black troops being raised from the Empire State, but just who "Captain Simmons and Hawkins" were in 1855 remains elusive.[10]

Nell's quote from the *New York Tribune* is not specific as to month or date of the article, so efforts thus far have not located the original newspaper piece. If other New York City papers made note of these volunteer companies, they, too, have eluded my rediscovery.[11] Yet Nell's account cannot be discounted because, interestingly enough, other states were seeing the formation of colored companies in the 1850s. For example, in Rhode Island, around 1855, "A colored company, called the 'National Guard, . . . (formed) in Providence, using by special grant, the State arms" while in Cincinnati, Ohio, sometime between 1854 and 1855, "A colored military company . . . (formed) They have chose the appropriate historic name of 'Attucks Guard.' On July 25, 1855 Miss Mary A. Darnes, in behalf of an association of ladies, presented the company with a flag . . ."[12]

Were New York City's black citizens trying to raise similar companies of black volunteers, especially during the 1850s? I believe they were despite the negative reactions of New York City authorities and of New York State's governor. Period records indicate that by the middle of the nineteenth century, the State of New York saw distinct divisions within its population's attitudes on the question of slavery and of the status of African-Americans living in New York. Abolitionists, for the most part, were strong in the western, central, and northern New York State, but in the city of New York, pro-slavery sentiments and anti-black feelings ran high. New York City's mayor, Fernando Wood, openly attacked the black man as inferior while city representatives even opposed the Thirteen Amendment to the Constitution when proposed. In 1850–1862 the city was still one of the principal ports for the outfitting of slave ships involved in the illegal trade to Africa.[13]

Although the Union League Club of New York City did help to energetically recruit black men for the 54th Massachusetts Volunteer Infantry and the 20th and 26th United States Colored Troops from 1863 to 1865, the New York City draft riots of 1863 dramatically showed the latent anti-black sentiments present within the city, especially with regard to arming black men as United States soldiers. As an example of such anti-black feeling, see George Templeton Strong's diary for October 2, 1863, concerning the famous charge of the 54th Massachusetts Volunteer Infantry at Fort Wagner, South Carolina.[14] It is not difficult, then, to project that New York's municipal authorities would not have looked favorably on the formation of these companies of colored men in 1854 and

1855, based upon the evidence revealed from 1854 through 1862. As a result, the "Hannibal Guards," the "Free Soil Guards," and the "Attucks Guards" were probably nothing more than failed attempts by the New York City's black citizens to form into volunteer militia organizations.

Another failed endeavor to create independent black militia companies transpired in New York City in May 1861. As had black volunteers in Pittsburgh, Pennsylvania, black volunteers in New York City began to drill in a privately hired drill hall, in order to prepare themselves for voluntary military service. The police informed the black New Yorkers that they would have to disband because the police could not ensure their safety from angry crowds opposed to the military drills of these black men. Even though their efforts were rebuffed by the municipality, by late July 1861 the city's black residents still offered to raise three regiments of volunteers. When this offer was presented to Governor Edwin D. Morgan, that proposal was not accepted either.[15]

To sum up at this point, attempts to form volunteer black militia companies in the New York City area from 1854 to 1862 came to naught. Despite the strong desire of black citizens to form volunteer companies, they were not allowed to become a part of the city's militia force or to form volunteer regiments for federal service.

At the state level, Governor Horatio Seymour, a Democrat elected in the fall of 1863 was an anti-Lincoln politician who opposed the recruitment of black troops within the state.[16] The New York State Militia, which changed its name to the National Guard, State of New York in 1862, had no segregated black militia company sanctioned between 1854 and 1866.[17] Other states did have separate militia companies, such as Rhode Island's Bristol Colored Infantry and Massachusetts "Shaw Guards," the 14th Unattached Company, Massachusetts Volunteer Militia during 1861–1865, but New York State did not.[18]

If undertakings took place outside New York City, say in Buffalo, Rochester, or Syracuse, which had sufficient black populations to support independent companies, they have not yet, to my knowledge, been uncovered.[19] These rejections by New York State authorities toward the formation of segregated militia companies are ironic since, at the New York State Convention of the Soldiers of 1812, held in 1854, a motion was passed asking the United States Congress to provide the surviving veterans and their widows with an annuity specifying "that such provisions should extend to and include both the Indian and African race . . . who enlisted or served in that war, and who joined with the white man in defending our rights and . . . independence."[20]

Black New Yorkers' efforts, especially in New York City, to join the state's militia or federal volunteers did not cease in light

A sketch of a corporal, Company B, 26th United States Colored Troops, circa 1864–1865, by Alan Archambault. (*Original in the Anthony Gero Collection*)

of the failures of 1854–1861. By July 1861 the great abolitionist, Frederick Douglass, based in Rochester, called upon New York State to recruit black men for the fight to save the Union and to end slavery. He felt there were enough volunteers of freemen in the state to do so and thundered such sentiments in speeches and publications. Douglass spoke adamantly that in this great crusade, the black man must fight and bleed to prove his worth in the ultimate victory and to secure his status as citizens for the future. He came to Cooper Union in February of 1862 and spoke on this theme to a largely white audience while, from September 1862 through March 1863, Reverends Henry Highland Garnet and James W. C. Pennington, famous New York City African-Americans, used the Shiloh Presbyterian Church and the Cooper Institute for public addresses that favored emancipation and the recruitment of African-American soldiers.[21]

Prominent New Yorkers with last names like Astor, Bacon, Beekman, Bliss, Cannon, Cowdin, Coyles, Fish, Jay, Ludington, Roosevelt, Van Rensselaer, Wadsorth, and Wetmore lent support to the recruitment of the 20th Regiment, United States Colored Troops.[22] In the case of one unsung volunteer, William Wise, a freedom seeker who escaped from Maryland and settled in the Auburn, Cayuga County, New York, circa 1860, he enlisted in the 54th Massachusetts Volunteer Infantry.[23] Frederick Douglass' sons, Charles and Lewis H. Douglass, also enlisted and the latter became the 54th's original sergeant-major. Hundreds of freemen of color flocked to enlist in the 54th, as did a forty-five man contingent from Little Falls, New York. Eventually the regiment's combat record from Fort Wagner in South Carolina to Olustee in Florida was second to none.[24]

Although black regiments, like the 20th, 26th, and 31st U.S.C.T. were assigned to New York State, they did not bear the name "New York Volunteers" but carried the Federal title of "United States Colored Troops," which shows some of the latent anti-black feeling in the state, which resisted labeling these black

New Yorkers as "New York Volunteers." However in Massachusetts, Governor John Andrew would not let the name of U.S.C.T.
be assigned to regiments of black men designated as volunteers
from Massachusetts. That is why the 54th Regiment, Massachusetts
Volunteer Infantry, the 55th Regiment, Massachusetts Volunteer
Infantry, and the 5th Regiment, Massachusetts Volunteer Cavalry,
never received the federal title of U.S.C.T. This was not the case,
however, for black regiments raised primarily from New York State
during the war such as the 20th, 26th, and 31st U.S.C.T.[25]

It should be noted that the designation of U.S.C.T. was one of
great pride for the men who served in it. Today their descendants
view their ancestors' service with equal honor and their legacy and
of their white officers, many of whom had abolitionist sentiments,
has great significance.[26]

Once New York State allowed the recruitment of men of
color, volunteers came in to help fill not only part of the 54th
Massachusetts Volunteer Infantry, but the 20th, 26th, and 31st
U.S.C.T. assigned by federal authorities to be raised in the Empire
State. Some men born in New York State choose to join other
regiments raised outside of the Empire State, like the 1st or 8th
U.S.C.T.[27] In January 1864, as the Union Club League presented
the new regimental flag to the 26th U.S.C.T., the regiment was
formed up in a formation to receive this gracious gift. A New
York City paper describes this presentation, in part:

> ... (the color was) a beautiful blue silk banner, trimmed
> with gold on which were inscribed the words 'Unconditional
> Loyalty,' ... Mr. Colyer then presented through the Chaplain
> a handsome satin rosette and badge, with the words 'Uncondi-
> tional Loyalty to God and our Country-To the Soldiers of the
> 26th United States Colored Troops-From their Friends' ... the
> regiment numbers a full thousand rank and file. They are a fine
> looking set of men, physically, we think they are superior to the
> 20th Colored regiment, which left three weeks since ...[28]

Black Canadians crossed the border to join the 54th Massachusetts. George Cooper, Benjamin Grimmidge, killed at Fort Wagner in 1863, and Thomas Younger, all are listed in William Wise's Company G. Other Black Canadians appear in various companies of the 54th as well.[29]

Contemporary newspaper accounts show African-American recruitment centers set up in New York City, Elmira, Albany, Syracuse, Buffalo, Rome, Oswego, and Auburn, to mention a few.[30] Many New Yorkers are listed in Emilio's history, too. For a sample, in Company A, Anthony Benton of Hudson served, as did Richard Foster from Troy, killed at Honey Hill while serving in Company C. In Company D, Issac Hawkins of Medina was captured at Olustee when the 54th made its valiant stand to save the Union forces hard pressed by enemy action. In Company F, Frederick Bond from Binghamton was wounded at Fort Wagner. Stephen A. Swails, from Elmira, was a 1st Sergeant in Company F. He received an officer's commission in March 1864 from Massachusetts' Governor Andrews and was one of the few black line officers in the Civil War. For his actions, Swails was cited for his "coolness and bravery, and efficiency" at the Battle of Olustee in Florida. Finally there is Alfred Cornish, Company F, who settled in Weeksville and who lived into the first two decades of the 20th century.[31]

William Wise's enlistment from Auburn is noteworthy when coupled with that of Harriet Tubman who had settled there prior to 1860, with the assistance of Auburnian William H. Seward, former governor of New York State and President Lincoln's Secretary of State. During the war, Tubman served as a volunteer nurse and scout for the Union forces, having gone down to the South Carolina coast in 1862. As a military scout, she provided valuable assistance to local commanders on several expeditions and, as such, received grateful praise from the federal government. Since her 1913 death, her residence, just outside of Auburn, has been a African-American cultural mecca.[32]

Several county studies have been written to document New York's black citizens in the U.S.C.T. Donald M. Wisoski's book on Oneida County's black soldiers and Harry Bradshaw Matthews' work on Delaware and Otsego Counties men in the U.S.C.T. are two good examples.[33] The span of African-American life in historic Weeksville in Brooklyn provides insights in black New Yorkers lives, as does Yellin's work, on the role of African-American women during the war.[34] As more research is conducted, one can expect that additional studies will be published. One area that needs exploration is the "integrated" Grand Army of the Republic posts that may be found in Cazenovia and perhaps in Dansville and Sandy Creek, New York, in the post–Civil War period.[35]

At a 2004 military exhibition at the Cayuga Museum in Auburn, a previously obscured photograph was on exhibit that presented

A drawing, based upon a photograph, of an African-American seaman in the United States Navy, ca. 1863–1865 by Barry E. Thompson. *(Anthony Gero Collection)*

the last Civil War veterans of that county alive in 1923. Their portrait showed eight aged and proud veterans, one of whom was an African-American, William Prue, who had enlisted in Company G, 26th U.S.C.T., and had resided in Cayuga County at the time of his enlistment. Shortly after the 1923 image was taken, Prue died and was buried in Oakglen Cemetery, Ledyard, Cayuga County.[36]

Conclusion

After the draft riots in New York City had ended, black New Yorkers from all regions of the state flocked to the colors in even greater numbers. By war's end more than 4,125 had enlisted from the Empire State.[37] Black sailors served in the Union Navy.[38] The probability that black New Yorkers were aboard many ships as crewmen is very good. In a *New York Tribune* article of September 8, 1865, one can catch a feeling of what had been contributed by black soldiers in the Civil War and of what it meant: "It is not too much to say that if this Massachusetts Fifty fourth had faltered when its trial came, two hundred thousand colored troops for whom it was a pioneer would never have been put into the field . . . But it did not falter. It made Fort Wagner such a name to the colored race as Bunker Hill has been for ninety years to the white Yankees."[39]

Among those thousands of black troops raised during the war, many from New York State served in the 54th Massachusetts, while others did duty in New York State's 20th, 26th, and 31st U.S.C.T. These men had risked much for the cause of emancipation and liberty but, as was often the reality in New York State, revisionism rose and obscured their military accomplishments. In the postwar years, attempts to besmirch the legacy of New York's black veterans would be made. Let this item on the funeral procession of President Lincoln held in New York City, on April 25, 1865, whose black marches were led by the Reverend James W.C. Pennington foreshadow the years that were to come. On April 26, 1865, the *New York Daily Tribune* reported that:

A small delegation of colored men marched in the rear of the
funeral process yesterday, well guarded by a detachment of police.
The precaution was a proper one, though, as the result proved,
quite unnecessary, judging from the reception they received along
the line of march. At various points, and particularly in Fifth
ave., ladies greeted the black men with waving of handkerchiefs,
thus emphatically marking their respect for the dead, who, as the
banner carried by those men said, was 'The Emancipator.' . . . The
sincerity of their mourning, and the propriety of it, was unques-
tioned, except by the Aldermen, some of whom, it is reported,
refused to take part in a procession where colored men were
allowed to show themselves. . . .

When the colored people passed the Union League Club in
the procession they all raised their hats in token of their respect
for a body most dear to them. . . .[40]

As those black New Yorkers marched last in the parade, "well
guarded under police protection," one wonders what must have
gone through their minds? In front of the Union League Club, in
a gesture of appreciation, they raised their hats, but what hopes for
the future did they have? Unhappily, the Empire State was about
to enter decades of the continued exclusion of her black citizens
from the National Guard. As the next chapter's title suggests,
"Everywhere but New York," reactionary undercurrents would keep
black New Yorkers from joining the State's National Guard, as if
the events from 1863 through 1865 had never happened. Not until
1916 would a segregated regiment of the Empire State's National
Guard be formally accepted. Even when it was, as in 1781, or
1814, or 1863, it took major national events to force such measures.
Whatever the reasons for the omission of black New Yorkers from
their State's National Guard, it can only be called shameful. Fearful
state authorities lacked the moral courage to reward the military
service of black Civil War veterans even in segregated units in the
state. For New York's black citizens, the years from 1866 to 1915
were to be dismal for military service in their own state.

Chapter 3

Everywhere, but New York, 1866–1915

After the Civil War, what would be the status of black soldiers in the Regular Army and various state militias and national guards and, in particular, the Empire State? Under pressure by the Radical Republicans and prominent African-Americans, the federal government did acknowledge the role of the U.S.C.T. in helping to preserve the Union and in keeping it safe in the postwar years. For example, among the Regular troops sent to Texas to help expel Napoleon III's intervention in the internal politics of Mexico was the Army of the Potomac's XXV Army Corps. This corps was an U.S.C.T. formation and now was assigned to help the United States enforce the Monroe Doctrine in a demonstration of force, along the Rio Grande.[1]

In the Regular Army's authorizations for 1866, several colored infantry and cavalry regiments were organized. In the 1869 reorganization of the army, these black regiments were consolidated into the 24th and 25th United States Infantry, and the 9th and 10th United States Cavalry. From 1868 until well into the 1890s, the exploits of these four regiments were of heroic proportions,

An Ordnance Sergeant in Full Dress Uniform, 24th Regiment, United States Infantry, ca. 1888–1897, a water color by Barry E. Thompson. *(Anthony Gero Collection)*

with fourteen Congressional Medals of Honor and more than thirty other Certificates of Merit and Orders of Honorable Mention earned by black soldiers.[2] As Howard University professor Rayford W. Logan states in, *The Betrayal of the Negro from Rutherford B. Hayes to Woodrow Wilson*: "Negroes had little, at the turn of the century to help sustain our faith in ourselves except the pride that we took in the Ninth and Tenth Cavalry, the Twenty-fourth and Twenty-fifth Infantry. . . . They were our Ralph Bunche, Marian Anderson, Joe Louis, and Jackie Robinson."[3]

The United States Military Academy at West Point began accepting black cadets in 1870. However, from 1870 to 1889, only three black cadets made it through: Henry O. Flipper (1877), John Hanks Alexander (1887), and Charles Young (1889). The status of all these cadet pioneers was perilous, and after 1889, it would be a while before another black cadet appeared there.[4] As far as I can document, all the appointments in this period were from outside of New York State, and there were no appointments of black New Yorkers to the academy in these years.

The United States Naval Academy accepted black midshipmen starting in 1872, but the record there was even worse than at West Point. From 1872 to 1935 no black midshipmen made it through the Naval Academy and were commissioned. In 1936 a black midshipman was appointed, but not until 1949 would a black midshipman finally graduate from that naval institution.[5]

The seagoing navy still maintained a level of integration in this era, and, with a major naval facility at the Brooklyn Navy Yard, it would seem reasonable to assume that black New Yorkers enlisted. Five Medal of Honors (MOH) were presented to black sailors before the Spanish-American War. For example, on December 26, 1872, Seaman Joseph B. Noil, of the U.S.S. *Ponhatan,* saved the life of Boatswain J.C. Walton who had fallen overboard. For his heroic action Noil was awarded the MOH. Regrettably, by 1903 naval authorities had undertaken a new tack and the past integration of crews and naval ratings was strongly restricted. From 1903 to 1914, if a black sailor was on aboard a naval vessel, he was usually relegated to the duties of a messman.[6]

With regard to the United States Coast Guard, called the Revenue Marine Service from 1867 to 1898, there are intriguing indications that from 1900 to 1916, some crews may have been integrated.[7] If black New Yorkers were in the Coast Guard in the years after the Civil War, more research has to be uncovered to verify their services, if, indeed, it happened at all.

As for the various state militias and national guards, the record is mixed. From 1868 through 1876, black militia units can be found in the Radical Republican state governments set up in the South, but these units were eventually eradicated by the late 1870s. The level of resistance to the Radical Republican administrations in the South and to black militia units that formed, by some white southerners, can remind one of what occurred in the former Yugoslavia in the late twentieth century. As an example, consider what transpired to a colored militia unit, Company A, 18th Regiment, South Carolina Militia, organized in 1874 in the Town of Hamburg. On July 4, 1876, the company's drill hall was attacked by armed white men and during the night of July 5, members of the colored company were executed by white vigilantes.[8]

After the Centennial of 1876, and with the 1877 Compromise that brought President Rutherford Hayes to the presidency, mostly Democrat Party administrations had been installed in the South. These state governments maintained white dominance in politics and entrenched segregated lifestyles culturally. In the late 1880s and into the 1890s, tensions relaxed and, as a result, segregated units of African-Americans in some southern states can be documented. For example, colored companies formed in Georgia, Alabama, Louisiana, Florida, and Virginia. Even in the District of Columbia as far back as 1869, colored units were created and maintained right up through to World War I.[9]

In the 1880s in the West and on the Pacific Coast, one finds segregated black militia units. In Colorado, the Capital Guards of Denver formed in about 1883, and a colored company may have been in San Francisco in the early 1870s.[10] In the mid-West, Ohio, Indiana, and Illinois had segregated black militia and national guard units during the 1880s and 1890s. Some of these units would serve in the Spanish-American War and World War I, such as the 8th Illinois, the 9th Ohio, and the 23rd Kansas Regiments.[11]

Pennsylvania had separate black national guard regiments between 1870 and 1873.[12] Rhode Island, 1863–1900, had various

African-American military formations while Connecticut, by 1879, had the 5th Battalion (Colored), Connecticut National Guard, all of whose officers were African-Americans. In Massachusetts, as early as 1865, the "Fourteenth Unattached Company, Massachusetts Volunteer Militia (Shaw Guards, colored)" had formed. In the early 1870s there may have been a black battalion in Massachusetts' militia, but by the 1890s only Company L, a totally African-American company within the 6th Regiment, M.V.M., a white command, existed.[13]

But what of New York State? Here the record is murky. There appears to have been attempts in the New York City area to have independent black military units in the early 1870s. Records show references to the Skidmore Guards and Lincoln Guards in New York City in the 1870s, but they were never officially made a part of the New York's military forces. As Colonel DeWitt Clinton Falls, the preeminent historian of New York's National Guard, wrote in his outline history of the 369th Infantry (formerly the 15th Regiment, National Guard, New York):

> This (regiment) was the first colored unit of the N.G. Though there had been several colored organizations among the independent military companies that existed in the city (of New York) from time to time. Among these the best known were the Skidmore and Lincoln Guards, both of which were disbanded when the State prohibited the bearing of arms by any organization not regularly a part of the N.G. or its auxiliary reserves...[14]

From Fall's statement, it seems that the Skidmore Guards and Lincoln Guards might have been relegated to rifle clubs or fraternal groups by skittish state and local authorities. Research in the *New York Times* indicate that the Skidmore Guards made an effort to become an official part of the state's military forces. A column called "Military Gossip," which regularly reported on aspects of the states' military forces, for Sunday, March 12, 1871, on page 6, column 2, states:

.... A card has recently been issued by two colored gentlemen of this City, announcing the organization of a colored military company to be known as the 'Skidmore Guard.' The command already numbers over one hundred members who are all honest, industrious and sober colored citizens ... The Skidmore Guard numbers among its members veterans of the Twentieth New York and Fifty-fourth Massachusetts regiments, which won bloody laurels on many a well-fought field. The company meets every Thursday evening at Washington Hall, No. 1, 370 Broadway, between Thirty-seventh and Thirty-eight streets. The Skidmore Guard is viewed as the nucleus of a more extensive colored military organization, which will not be formed merely with the idea of making an ostentatious display of gorgeous uniforms in public thoroughfares, but for thorough instruction in military science and discipline, and with the intention of affording the authorities all proper aid in time of emergency. This movement ought to be a successful one, and we trust Capt. Charles F. Leslie will persevere in his undertaking. . . .

The *New York Times* on April 16, 1871, page 6, column 4, ran an article entitled "Tammany Negroes-Another Scheme for Catching the Colored Vote-A Negro Regiment to be Raised by Tweed & Co," which heralded the formation and proposed uniforms for a regiment called the "Griffin Excelsior Guards." However, the unit's links to the Tweed Democratic Party machine may have been cause for the unit's rejection by local African-American groups.[15]

Finally, a city black unit in 1876 called the Veteran Guards, under a Major James B. Lee, has to undergo more research, as do the Shaw Cadets, reportedly formed from city students circa 1863 and named for the colonel of the 54th Massachusetts Volunteers. Unfortunately by 1877, many white New York City residents sympathy and support towards the black population had waned.[16]

Upstate New York also saw African-Americans who wished to form military groups in the post–Civil War period. One such example was the Onondaga Colored Battalion established in 1876.

During the United States' Centennial year, the *Syracuse Journal* ran a series of articles about the formation of this black battalion.[17] In a pamphlet on the early history of black Syracusans, it stated that on February 21, the *Syracuse Journal* reported that a George W. Berryman, an Onondaga County cigar manufacturer, had been elected the colonel of a black battalion composed of "3 companies of 30 men each and a drum corps . . ." with colonel and staff to be white men.[18] The city of Syracuse had a large number of citizens, as did Onondaga County, who had served in the Civil War in the 54th Massachusetts. Whether these men remained in the area to help form this new battalion, after 1865, has not been verified.

On May 11, 1876, the *Syracuse Journal* reported that the battalion had received Springfield rifles. By October 2, the paper reported that, "There are now enrolled in the battalion nearly 100 of our worthiest young colored men, . . . who are becoming quite proficient in the manual (of arms)." By August 25, 1877, the *Syracuse Journal* reported that the "Onondaga Colored Battalion, Captain William H. Franklin," had participated in a large sham battle in Syracuse. Records indicate that Franklin was a waiter at the Vanderbilt Hotel, which may suggest that he was an African-American. There is no William H. Franklin listed in Emilio's work on the 54th Massachusetts, but Franklin could have served in another U.S.C.T. regiment and then have gone back to the Syracuse area to live. By December 17 the paper stated that the company was drilling at rooms on Chestnut Street but hinted that interest in the unit was lagging. From this point in time, mention of the battalion disappears from local papers, at least as far as I can document.

However, another Syracuse paper, the *Syracuse Courier* along with the *Syracuse Journal*, each carried stories on August 5, 1880, about the band of the Palmer Guards, but they do not say who these guards were. Just who the Palmer Guards were might be revealed in a Geneva, New York paper, the *Courier*. On August

15th, 1881, it ran an article that reported the Palmer Guards "attracted much attention for the soldierly bearing of its members and the excellent drill ... It was quite a novelty, as with the exception of New York city, where there are two or three, we know of no military company of colored men in the State." Thus, had the earlier Onondaga Colored Battalion evolved into the Palmer Guards to which this band was now attached?

What we do know is that the Onondaga Colored Battalion attempted to form in 1876 and was still active in 1877 as a military command, perhaps in preparation of joining the Empire State's military forces. When it became obvious that the State would not accept them into the National Guard, it seems reasonable to assume that battalion evolved into the Palmer Guards in about 1880 or 1881. Neither of these units was accepted into New York State's military forces and, by the late 1880s or early 1890s, had faded into obscurity or had evolved into a band providing martial music for the African-American communities in the area.

If any of these independent black units, in the New York City area or in the Syracuse region, had been placed, even as segregated units, into New York State's National Guard, records would have indicated that and historians like Colonel DeWitt Clinton Falls would have noted it, but no such action took place. Despite the legacy of service of black New Yorkers in the U.S.C.T. and in the Massachusetts regiments, and in light of the fact that many of these veterans still resided in New York State, no officially sanctioned black companies, battalions, or regiments were allowed. From 1866 to 1898 a color line was maintained in the New York's military forces, which no state authority was willing to destroy.

When war with Spain finally exploded, black New Yorkers wanted to join and serve. Other states permitted segregated units to form. Virginia, Alabama, Illinois, Ohio, North Carolina, and Kansas all had such organizations. For example, the 8th Illinois went in as a full regiment with black officers, from colonel down

to lieutenants, while Kansas formed 23rd Kansas Volunteers. Both
of these regiments were sent to Cuba during the war.

Massachusetts created the 6th Regiment, Massachusetts Volunteer Infantry, whose regimental structure was unique because it
was composed of nine white companies, and one black company,
Company L. When the regiment arrived at Camp Alger in Virginia, the federal government tried to take out Company L and
assign it to another all-black volunteer regiment. The entire 6th
Regiment, with the backing of Massachusetts governor, would have
no part of such a move. For its entire service, the 6th Regiment
was organized as nine white companies and one black company,
all of whom were Massachusetts volunteers.[19]

A Corporal in Full Dress, 24th Regiment, United States Infantry, ca. 1902, a water
color by Barry E. Thompson. *(Anthony Gero Collection)*

Amazingly, with these precedents from other states before them, New York State did not form any black volunteer units during the War of 1898. Even when patriotic black New Yorkers asked New York's Governor Frank S. Black to accept them as volunteers, he refused, explaining that the color line in the National Guard of the state was traditional and was still to be maintained. The official records of New York State during this short war are painful to review, but facts are stubborn things, and the record speaks clear. From 1898 to 1899, no volunteer black units from the Empire State were created.[20]

If black New Yorkers served in the United States Army from 1898 until 1916, they must have done so as individuals. For example, between 1908 to 1912, the Army's 24th Infantry Regiment was stationed at posts in Buffalo, Oswego, and at Madison Barracks, near Watertown, New York. It would have been possible for black New Yorkers to have enlisted in those years, as the regiment must have recruited in the state. Opportunities to join their own state's national guard did not exist in this period, although contemporary photographs sometimes show black New Yorker's with local military units, but usually as company stewards or servants.[21]

It is interesting to note that Cornell University in Ithaca, New York, had a cadet corps, formed as early as the 1870s. In an undated photograph, which still hangs on the walls at the cadet center at Barton Hall on the Cornell campus, the band of the cadet corps, circa 1900, is preserved. One of the bandsmen is an African-American, but who he was is still being researched. What the image suggests though is that Cornell's cadet corps may have been integrated sometime between 1900 and 1910.[22]

Conclusion

Winds of change were building in New York, and that emphasis came, in great part, due to a growing population coming from the south. Between 1900 and 1920, "two out of every three New York State residents who migrated from south of the Mason and Dixon Line were nonwhite. This northward movement gained impetus after 1900 . . ."[23] This great migration was not just confined to New York State. Many of these southern blacks settled in the metropolitan areas of the country, such as Chicago.[24] In the case of New York State, the main area for their settlement was New York City. As a result, the state's growing African-American population would make itself felt in the next decades, much as they had influenced the period of 1789 through 1812.[25] With regard to their involvement in New York's National Guard, this would finally mean the creation of a black regiment between 1913 and 1916.

The great migration of black Americans from the rural south to the industrial north was, in part, prompted by American industrialists who sought new laborers for their plants. Another reason for this migration, according to some historians, was the treatment by southern whites toward African-Americans after the compromise of 1877.[26] Whatever the reasons, southern blacks left and headed up to the north where the hope of better treatment and jobs seemed to exist. It was the prospect of a better life that fueled this migration, but would such hopes be achieved, and how would this burgeoning black population impact New York's National Guard?

First, Woodrow Wilson's election and initial administration offered a mixed bag for African-Americans. Initially, they were attracted to him, especially by his statement that he would give them "absolute fair dealings, for everything by which I could assist in advancing the interests of their race in the United States."[27] He even carried on the tradition of allowing the Washington High School Cadets, an African-American unit, to march in the inaugural parade, but Wilson raised no objections when Postmaster General Albert S. Burleson widened the segregation practices in the federal government in 1913, and when a black delegation called at the White House to protest this action, Wilson found their language insulting.[28]

Second, in the United States Congress many discriminatory bills were proposed during the early Wilson administration. One proposal attempted to exclude blacks from being officers in the Army or Navy while another wanted to exclude immigrants to the United States of "Negro descent."[29] In both instances the Wilson administration did not attempt to block either proposal.

Third, by 1915 the president ordered the occupation of Haiti by United States Marines, which was loudly protested by African-Americans at the time. Also in that year the blatantly racist film *Birth of a Nation* was released and the famous African-American leader, Booker T. Washington died. As the next chapter will reveal, none of these actions and events were to stop the pressure for change building up in New York State's African-American communities, especially in regard to their desired service in the Empire State's national guard.[30]

From 1900 to 1915 the status quo in the Empire State's National Guard would be maintained, but, as the war clouds crossed the Atlantic in 1914, America would be challenged by a conflict of global proportions, much as it had from 1807 to 1815. The impact of this new European discord would eventually see persons of African descent living in New York State called to serve, and serve they did, in the thousands. Some even volunteered to help the Allied Powers as early as 1914, such as Eugene Jacques Bullard who enlisted in the French Foreign Legion in that year.[31]

In 1916 the old color line in New York State would be crossed. On October 1, 1916, the segregated 15th Regiment Infantry of New York's National Guard was presented their regimental flags by Governor Charles Whitman. For black New Yorkers a measure of participation in their state's national guard was formally achieved, based upon a legislative process begun, officially, in 1913.[32]

Chapter 4

A Lost Opportunity, New York's Black Soldiers, 1916–1918

The year 1916 would be monumental for black New Yorkers' participation in its National Guard, but to understand the significance, one needs to examine some events of that year. The United States was a racially charged nation, primed to explode in violence against African-Americans. Internationally, violence threatened American neutrality. For example, in 1916 a black man had been publicly burned to death in Waco, Texas; while in South Carolina, a mob had killed another African-American. In Mexico, due to America's intervention, twenty-two troopers of the Army's famous black Tenth Cavalry had been killed in action. Meanwhile, the European War threatened a neutral America, especially by Imperial Germany's use of the U-boats in the Atlantic Ocean.[1]

When the United States Congress finally declared war in April 1917, the majority of African-Americans believed that this new conflict provided a chance to finally end the colored line. After war was declared wild rumors swept the South of a German plot to set the country ablaze with black insurrections, helping to fuel a new round of lynching and terrorism. Yet, despite this increased domestic violence, many in the African-American communities felt that a foreign war was "a God-sent blessing" that would earn them the respect of white Americans through valiant wartime service. As a result, the Central Committee of Negro College Men was formed and met with President Wilson to establish special officer training camps for black officers for the proposed black regiments, then being raised in the expanded Federal Army.[2]

On July 28, 1917, fifteen thousand African-Americans marched on Fifth Avenue in New York City to protest the continued discriminations against persons of color. A leaflet, handed out that day, stated:

> . . . We march because we want to make impossible a repetition of Waco, Memphis, and East St. Louis by arousing the conscience of the country, and to bring the murderers of our brothers, sisters, and innocent children to justice. We march because we deem it a crime to be silent in the face of such barbaric acts. We march because we are thoroughly opposed to Jim Crow cars, segregation, discrimination, disfranchisement, lynchings and the host of evils that are forced on us . . . We march because we want our children to live in a better land and enjoy fairer conditions than have fallen our lot . . ."[3]

Finally, after a racial incident in Texas on August 13 directed toward the 3rd Battalion, of the famous 24th Infantry Regiment, and due to the urgings of Robert R. Moton of the Tuskegee Institute, with the assistance of prominent philanthropist Julius Rosenwald, Secretary of War Newton D. Baker held a conference of "men interested in the Negro Question." From this dialogue came the appointment of Emmett J. Scott.[4] On October 5, Scott, who had for eighteen years been the secretary to Booker T. Washington, was designated Special Assistant to Secretary Baker and was to serve as "confidential advisor in matters affecting the interests of the ten million Negroes in the United States and the part they are to play in connection with the present war."[5]

At the national level, in April 1917 there had been only 750,000 men in the Regular Army and National Guard, of whom approximately ten thousand were African-Americans. Segregated National Guard units existed in Illinois, Ohio, Maryland, Connecticut, Massachusetts, Tennessee, and the District of Columbia and now New York, but many southern states had eliminated their former black guard units, which had been created in the 1870s and maintained into the 1890s.[6] Black Americans could not join the United States Marine Corps, and their role in the Navy was limited, although by war's end, thirty black women served as naval yeomanettes. Other black women served in the American Expeditionary Forces as secretaries or YMCA workers, such as Mrs. Helen Curtis of New York City. Some women of color even served as nurses.[7]

When the national draft was instituted, although 10 percent of the total population was black, 13 percent of the draftees were men of color. One out of five African-Americans who were sent to France saw combat, while in the American Expeditionary Forces (AEF), as a whole, two out of three white soldiers took part in battle.[8] What these statistics show is that, although drafted in greater proportion to the general population, black soldiers would see limited combat based upon racial attitudes in the Army.

Commissioned black officers experienced discrimination also because, traditionally, officers are viewed as "officers and gentlemen" so elevating African-Americans to such rank ran against segregationist practices. In the years before the war, black Americans had been barred from officer training programs, like the Plattsburg School; however, pressure from the black community help set up a segregated officer's school at Des Moines, Iowa, from June to October 1917, where at least eighteen New Yorkers graduated. Regrettably, this school commissioned few senior officers above the rank of captain, which would impact the 367th and 369th Infantry from New York State.[9]

The AEF's commander, General John J. Pershing, had experience with black soldiers in the Indian Wars and the Spanish-American War and generally favored their valor.[10] In his memoirs, Pershing stated: "My earlier service with colored troops in the Regular Army had left a favorable impression on my mind. In the field, on the frontier and elsewhere they were reliable and courageous . . . Under capable white officers and with sufficient training, negro soldiers have always acquitted themselves creditably . . ."[11] This statement is hardly a ringing endorsement of black soldiers, but nonetheless, it does show Pershing's willingness to use African-American soldiers whose reliability and courage he did not question. The latent prejudice of the caveat if led by "capable white officers and with sufficient training" would grow even stronger in the United States Army from 1917 and into 1918.

As units for the AEF were shipped overseas, the governments of Great Britain, France, and Italy put enormous pressure to fill out their hugely depleted forces by using American soldiers as replacements in their armies. Neither did the Allies desire to have a separate United States Army on the Western Front.[12] Although some individual black New Yorkers did enlist in the British Army, the British, although wanting American soldiers, were not receptive to African-American troops. Racial violence had broken out in England and Wales in 1917, involving British black colonial troops. Even as late as 1918, when Pershing requested that the 92nd Division (Colored), AEF be trained by the British, Lord Milner, British Minister of War, in a letter dated May 13, wrote his nation did not wish to "undertake the training of a colored Division . . ."[13]

The French, meanwhile, had had good experiences with their black West African troops so were more positive to American black soldiers.[14] As a result, a compromise was brokered where four regiments of African-American soldiers would be "temporarily"

A reconstruction of a private, 369th United States Infantry, 15/16 July 1918 in France armed with a captured German Mauser rifle by Raymond Johnson. *(Original in the Anthony Gero Collection)*

assigned to the French. One of these regiments was the 15th, now redesignated the 369th United States Infantry.[15]

At the same time, German propaganda was directed toward black Americans. According to John Hope Franklin, the "Germans made the most of these unfortunate incidents in their efforts to spread anti-war sentiment among the Negroes. They kept a careful record of lynchings and the attacks of whites on Negroes and urged Negroes to desert the struggle out of which they were gaining nothing..."[16] These domestic efforts, run by the German ambassador in Mexico, were primarily directed toward the South, but not exclusively.[17]

German efforts to create disloyalty among the Empire State's black citizens had grown so bad that on March 15, 1918, a New York citizen, Trumbull White, wrote George Creel, federal director

of the Committee on Public Information (CPI), that rumors in cir-
culation in Harlem, among the families of black servicemen then in
France, were very prevalent. White felt that, if unanswered, these
rumors would impact on the home front. White pleaded with Creel,
"Please do not think this matter a light one..."[18] As an example
of German sedition in New York State, on April 11, 1918, a Max
Freudenheim was arrested for an attempt on the life of a black
woman in Harlem who had turned him in as a German agent.
Upon investigation, Freudenheim stated that German agents had
promised that, if Germany won the war, a southern state would
be set aside as a black colony, exclusively for African-Americans'
use as "a Black Republic..."[19]

In 1918 domestic violence had become so bad that Secretary
of War Baker urged President Wilson to publicly denounce it in a

Sketch of a company grade officer, 367th United States Infantry, 92nd Division,
AEF, summer 1918 by Eric Manders. *(Original in the Anthony Gero Collection)*

written statement to the various state governors. President Wilson
wrote that "the unpatriotic character of these acts of brutality and
injustice" would be investigated by the Justice Department, in
conjunction with local authorities, to punish those involved. He
also felt that these acts "cannot live where the community does
not countenance it."[20]

Overseas, German propaganda was directed toward black
soldiers. Leaflets were dropped trying to convince them not to
fight. One "captured" leaflet's message was very direct:

> To the Colored Soldiers of the United States Army
> 'Hello boys, what are you doing over here? Fighting the Ger-
> mans? Why? Have they ever done you any harm? Of course
> some white folks and the lying English-American papers told
> you that the Germans ought to be wiped out for the sake of hu-
> manity and Democracy. What is Democracy? Personal freedom;
> all citizens enjoying the same rights as the white people do in
> America, . . . or are you not rather treated over there as second
> class citizens? Can you get into a restaurant where white people
> dine? Can you get a seat in a theatre where white people sit? . . .
> And how about the law? Is lynching . . . a lawful proceeding in
> a Democratic country? . . . [21]

Amazingly, despite all of these efforts to disrupt the loyalty of
America's black soldiers, their morale stayed high and their service
to the war effort did not slacken.[22] The black population, and in
particular New York's, would not be enticed toward sedition and
treason. Although it would be hard to ignore the racial discriminations of the period, black New Yorkers remained loyal and served
with distinction in France. Let these examples document the lost
opportunity of World War I for the Empire State: the service of
the 15th Regiment, New York, National Guard, which became the
369th United States Infantry; the role of the 367th United States
Infantry; and lastly, a brief case study of Cayuga County's African-
American community, home to Harriet Tubman and William

Seward. In each example, what might have been achieved from "the war to end all wars" can be witnessed.

Prior to World War I, an African-American New York City resident, Charles W. Fillmore, had attempted to have a black National Guard unit raised in the Empire State. Legislation was authorized on June 2, 1913, but no unit was formed. By 1916, in part due to the exploits of the Regular Army's 10th Cavalry in Mexico, and with the election of New York State Governor Charles S. Whitman, the 15th Infantry (Colored), was created and William Hayward was appointed colonel. Two hundred New York City residents, many with previous military service in the United States Regulars, immediately joined and provided the nucleus of the regiment's enlisted men.[23]

Hayward, son of United States Senator Monroe L. Hayward (Nebraska), had been a colonel in the 2nd Regiment of Infantry, Nebraska National Guard and a Republican Party leader, by 1908. He had moved to New York in 1910, opened a law office, and became active in politics. In 1914 and 1916 he had managed Whitman's campaign for governor, and, during Whitman's second term, was Public Service Commissioner when invited by the governor to organize the 15th Regiment.[24]

White and black men made up the 15th Regiment's officer corps. Many of the white officers were from National Guard units, eager to serve with this new black regiment. Some were Ivy Leaguers from Harvard, Yale, and Princeton, and one, Captain Hamilton Fish Jr. was the son of Hamilton Fish, speaker of the New York State Assembly, and great grandson of President Grant's Secretary of State Hamilton Fish. Some paid the ultimate sacrifice in war, such as 2nd Lieutenant Ernest H. Holden, killed in action while serving with the regiment in France.[25]

The African-American officers were from the "intellectual minority" of New York's black community. Lieutenant James R. Europe organized the regiment's band and was the only black officer left in the regiment by 1919. Another was Captain Napoleon Bonaparte Marshall, in civilian life a lawyer, seriously wounded in fighting at Metz, and transferred out of the unit in March of 1919, under AEF directives against black officers. The others were Captain Charles W. Fillmore, First Lieutenant George W. Lacey, and Second Lieutenant D. Lincoln Reid.[26]

From its formation, the 15th had a regimental élan. Several nicknames attached themselves in those early days, such as the "15th Heavy Foot" and "The Traveling 15th." Major Little referred to the men of his battalion as his "men of bronze."[27]

In 1917 the 15th was low in the number of officers to men, usually numbering two officers per company, instead of the six called for. It had supply problems with a shortage of uniforms, equipment, and weapons, although this was not an uncommon problem in America's expanding military forces. The regiment had no armory to drill in either, which hindered its training.[28] Lastly, no Regular Army noncommissioned officers from the 24th or 25th Infantry were transferred to train the 15th, neither were any Regular Army officers assigned, until after the Armistice in 1918.[29]

The regiment went into camp at Peekskill, New York in May 1917, where the men were given additional rifle practice, while also assuming guard duty at various military and civilian sites in New York and New Jersey. It was at this time that the regiment suffered its first war casualty when one of its soldiers was killed by a pro-German sympathizer. In another incident, guards of the 15th captured a German spy for whom "the secret service had been looking for sometime."[30]

While the regiment chafed at performing guard duty, other units from New York State were being sent off for further training, before being sent overseas. Formed from infantry regiments of New York's National Guard, the newly created 27th Division left to go to South Carolina, after a grand parade down Fifth Avenue, but the 15th was not allowed to go with them. When the 69th

Infantry, New York, National Guard paraded in New York City as a part of the 42nd Division, nicknamed the Rainbow Division, the 15th was not allowed to join in. When Colonel Hayward was informed of the reason why his regiment was not being sent with the Rainbow Division, he was told that it was because black was not a color of the rainbow. His response reportedly was "Damn their going away parade! We'll have a parade of our own when we come home—those of us who come home—and it will be a parade that will make history!" Hayward kept this promise, in grand style, when the regiment returned in February of 1919.[31]

Colonel Hayward now made the rounds of the military authorities, determined to get his regiment sent for more training. Ultimately, his efforts resulted in a directive that ordered the unit to Spartanburg, South Carolina, "to be attached to the 27th Division, for training . . ."[32]

At Spartanburg, several incidents illustrate what lost opportunities the service of the 15th with the 27th Division could have provided. While the regiment tried to be cordial with the local community, racial incidents developed. One of the more potentially dangerous involved Lieutenant Europe and Noble Sissle of the 15th, who had been turned away by a local hotel manager as they tried to buy a newspaper. When several white soldiers tried to intervene on behalf of these two soldiers, Europe commanded that all soldiers present should leave before violence broke out. Since other merchants near the 27th Division's training camp also refused to sell goods to men from the 15th, in a dramatic show of support, men from the 12th and 71st Regiments confronted those merchants and demanded that they either serve these black New Yorkers or close up their shops since ". . . They're our buddies. And we won't buy from the men who treat them unfairly."[33]

Unfortunately, local tensions would not subside. On October 24, 1917, the 15th Regiment was ordered shipped to France and was detached from the 27th Division. As the regiment headed out of camp to the train station, a spontaneous event happened that, if depicted in a movie, might be seen as a Hollywood moment. As Major Little wrote: "... as we swung along through the camps of the Twelfth, Seventy-first and Seventh Regiments, in the course of our hike, thousands of brave New York lads of the 27th Division lined the sides of the road-way, and sang us through, to the tune of *Over There* ..."[34]

What a grand sight that must have been and what a lost opportunity it was since the 15th was no longer attached to the 27th Division. What might have been achieved socially if the 15th, as a National Guard regiment, had stayed with the 27th Division? Would their service in combat in France with the 27th Division have helped to create a "band of brothers" that would have had profound influence in the post war years? I believe it would have, but the opportunity was lost.

With the 15th now headed for France, the question was what to do with them once there. General Pershing had three black National Guard regiments available to him then, but he could not, or would not, integrate them into any white divisions. Therefore, he formed these three regiments into the 93rd (Provisional) Division and attached a regiment of drafted black soldiers to complete its infantry structure. At first, Pershing wanted to use this division as Service of Supply troops or Pioneer Infantry, but under pressure from the Allied governments for American combat soldiers, he assigned all four black infantry regiments to the French Army.[35]

The assignment of these regiments let Pershing resolve two problems. First, it allowed him to placate an Allied Power; second, it helped remove a potential racial problem in the AEF. In his post war memoirs, Pershing stated:

> Very naturally, the four infantry regiments of the 93rd Division (colored) which had been assigned to the four French Divisions, were anxious to serve with our armies, and I made application for the organization and shipment of the rest of the division, but to no purpose and these regiments remained with the French to the end ...[36]

When the 15th arrived in France, it was redesignated as the 369th United States Infantry and would not serve with the American AEF in combat. Rather, the regiment would be assigned to the French Army, but not right away. At first, the 369th spent months on fatigue duty at Saint-Nazaire, at times harassed by Army officials who had "the spirit of the South," as one black officer put it.[37]

Local French authorities were different in their attitudes to these African-American soldiers, however. As one black officer of the 369th wrote, "I have never before experienced what it meant to be really free, to taste real liberty, in a phrase to be a man."[38] The humane reception by the French toward the 369th and other black American troops would eventually bring about a secret and infamous AEF memo to the French government to stop such civil and humanitarian fraternization.

With regard to the regiment's history in France, several other events must be considered. The first deals with the band tour, ordered by General Pershing as a morale booster for American servicemen, which helped make the 369th's band world famous, but which showed the latent discrimination in the AEF. Originally raised by Lieutenant Europe, the band had recruited musicians all across the nation and had obtained thousands of dollars in donations, even John D. Rockefeller had given $500. Before it was ordered on tour, it was rumored Europe was not going to be allowed to command because a white officer had to be in charge. Colonel Hayward would have no part of this indignity and managed, somehow, to have Europe stay in command during the tour.[39]

The second event involves the regiment's élan, as seen by the actions of regimental color bear Sergeant Cox of Major Dayton's battalion. As recounted in Little's history on pages 183–184, the regiment had entered the Zone of the Advance in April 1918. When enemy planes were sighted on the march to Remicourt, the unit was ordered to halt, fall out, and lie down, which was promptly

carried out, except for Sergeant Cox who bore the colors and who
stood on the road. When questioned as to why he refused cover,
he stated that he had promised Governor Whitman, back at the
Union League Club presentation of the regiment's colors, never to
let the flag droop in the dust.

On March 13, 1918, the 369th moved from St. Nazaire and
went to Givry-en-Argonne to become a part of the 16th Division,
8th Corps, 4th French Army, commanded by General Gouraud.
In April 1918 the regiment's reserve battalion was paraded before
French General Gouraud, a battle of Gallipoli veteran. On this
day, Sergeant Cox, without orders, dipped the National Standard
in salute to General Gouraud, feeling that George Washington
would have done the same.[40] Like the 54th Massachusetts in the
Civil War, the actions of the 369th would be reported in the press,
and so they were, which only heightened the 369th's élan. In mid-
April the regiment was given responsibility for a 4.5 kilometer
sector of the front. Although the 369th was less than 1 percent of
the American troops then in France, at this time it held 20 percent
of all territory assigned to American combat forces.[41]

Late in May an event happened that would gain the regiment
a combat reputation. While on observation post duty in the front
line trenches, Henry Johnson and Needham Roberts were attacked
by enemy trench raiders. Despite suffering severe wounds, Johnson,
a former railroad porter from Albany, drove off the Germans in
fierce hand-to-hand combat. In the process he killed at least four
of the raiders and may have wounded upward of thirty more. For
his brave deed, the French would award him the Croix de Guerre
with golden palm, signifying extraordinary valor.[42]

After the action, Major Little and a group of others explored
the site. From their inspection, it was obvious that Johnson had
killed one of the raiders by thrusting his bolo knife through the
man's pillbox cap and into his skull. Major Little retrieved this
grisly souvenir and when French General Le Gallaes, Chief of

Training, asked for the cap, it was sent to him. The general then had it framed and hung on his office wall as an example of a *"bon soldat."*[43]

The American press too reported on this fight. In the *Saturday Evening Post,* Irwin Cobb curiously wrote, "because we had grown accustomed to thinking of our negroes as members of labor battalions working along the lines of communication-unloading ships . . . but that the heroism of Johnson and Roberts would mean that n-i-g-g-e-r will merely be another way of spelling the word American."[44] The *Boston Post*, in an article entitled, "No Color Line There,' stated, "In the service of democracy there is no such distinction. General Pershing's late report places in the roll of honor the names of two soldiers of one of our colored regiments, Privates Johnson and Roberts . . . This is the true ideal of service. No matter what the color of skin, we all recognize it."[45]

In Pittsburgh, the *Chronicle Telegraph* quoted General Grant on the positive fighting ability of the Civil War black soldiers, and then made note of their service in the Indian Wars and Spanish-American War. The *Chronicle Telegram* went on to say, ". . . And now in France they are living up to the reputation they have won on other far distant fields." The exploits of Johnson and Roberts were also favorably reported on in the *Buffalo Evening News, Brooklyn Times*, the *New York Times,* and *New York Tribune.*[46]

Others of the 369th proved equally as valiant. In June 1918 the Germans launched their last great Western Front offensive. Helping to stop that enemy drive was Sergeant Bob Collins, who earned his Croix de Guerre for effective handling of his machine gun during heavy enemy action. Private Jefferson Jones, who manned an observation post during the same assault, sent a message back to his company officer, "I am being fired upon heavily from the left. I await your instructions. Trusting these few lines will find you the same, I remain yours truly, Jefferson Jones."[47]

By July, the 369th was attached to the French 161st Division, 4th French Army, and was assigned to the front facing Butte de

Mesnil, near Minancourt. After coming under heavy enemy fire while advancing more than six miles, the regiment got a newly coined motto, "God Damn, Let's Go." When ordered by French General Foch to attack an enemy bulge at the Marne, a black officer of the 369th, Captain Charles Fillmore, was officially commended in this attack for his calm leadership under fire.[48]

As a final example of the regiment's bravery and the cost of modern warfare in human terms, the Distinguished Service Cross was won by Corporal Elmer Earl of Company K and Private Elmer McCowin, also of Company K. In describing how he won his medal, Corporal Earl stated: "We had taken a hill on September 26 in the Argonne. We came to the edge of a swamp, when enemy machine guns opened fire. It was so bad that of fifty-eight of us who went into a particular strip, only eight came out without being killed or wounded. I made a number of trips out here and brought back about a dozen wounded men."[49]

As a result of these and other brave deeds, the Germans began referring to the soldiers of the 93rd Division as *"blutlustige schwartze Manner"* or "blood thirsty black men." The enemy also referred to the black American soldiers as "Hell Fighters," which pleased the French, who had nothing but praise for these American regiments assigned to their formations.[50]

Regrettably, AEF policies toward the 369th between May and November 1918 are hurtful to review. Combat soldiers were pulled out of the unit to serve as orderlies to General Pershing, pay was stopped to the entire regiment, except Company C, in May; and even special holiday rations at Thanksgiving and Christmas were not sent. Fortunately, the regimental officers did supply, from their own resources, special treats for their men on both holidays.[51]

The greatest slight was directed, I believe, toward the five black officers who had originally come over with the regiment. Eventually, these officers were transferred to the 92nd Division (Colored) AEF, despite Colonel Hayward's valiant efforts to keep them. As he wrote:

In August 1918 the American Expeditionary Force adopted the policy of having either all white or all colored soldiers with Negro regiments, and so ours were shifted away (though Lt. Europe was later returned to us as bandmaster, whereas he had been in the machine gun force before). Our colored officers were now in the July fighting and did good work, and I felt and feel now, that if colored officers are available and capable, they, and not white officers, should command colored troops. There is splendid material there. I sent away 42 sergeants in France who were commissioned officers in other units, but they declared they'd rather be sergeants in the Fifteenth than lieutenants or captains in other regiments.[52]

When the Armistice came, the *Stars and Stripes* had this to say about the 369th: "The farthest north at 11 o'clock (when the armistice went into effect) on the front of the two armies was held at the extreme American left, up Sedan way, by the troops of the 77th New York Division. The farthest east-the nearest the Rhine-was held by those New York soldiers who used to make up the 'old 15th New York' and have long been brigaded with the French. They were in Alsace and their line ran through Thann and across the railway that leads to Colmar . . ."[53]

In summary, the regiment's record was outstanding. It had remained under enemy fire for 191 days, without relief, and suffered 1,500 men killed and wounded. Within its ranks, 171 officers and men got either the Legion of Honor or the Croix de Guerre. Several were awarded the American Distinguished Service Cross. The regiment never lost a man through capture, or lost a trench, nor a foot of ground to the enemy. It had been "first to the Rhine" and was deserving of its title of "Hell Fighters."[54]

Back home, newspapers gave the regiment glowing praise. For example, the *Literary Digest*, on January 18, 1919, in an article entitled "Croix de Guerre and Rare Praise for American Negro Troops," pointed out the 369th's valiant efforts, while the *New York Evening Sun* stated that America's black soldiers had "proved their valor on countless occasions, and it was one of the common stories that Jerry feared the 'Smoked Yankees' more that any other troops he met."[55]

Unfortunately, despite its great combat record, the discriminatory practices of the United States Army would not go away. No amount of blood spilled or medals won would earn these proud black New Yorkers the equality they had hoped to gain from their service. As a final affront, when the regiment left France, Colonel Hayward did not feel it was safe for the regimental band to play as the 369th paraded down to the transport ship waiting to take them home. Only at the urging of the French port authorities, and once the regiment was safely aboard, did Colonel Hayward let the band give a final musical send off. In Colonel Hayward's defense, he would not let this last indignity be repeated when the regiment got home.

Once in New York City, the regiment had a parade of epic proportions. Passing by the reviewing stand on 5th Avenue, where Governor Al Smith stood, the regiment marched in massed formation. Playing French military music that rebounded off the buildings, Europe's band heralded the 369th's return. When the regiment turned up Lenox Avenue at 130th Street, the band struck up the song *Here Comes My Daddy*, to the shouts of thousands of joyous Harlem spectators.[56] Let Major Little have the last word on the 369th's history:

> The 15th Heavy Foot was a self-made regiment of the American Army. It started without tradition, without education, and without friends. In all its career it never had even one thoroughly equipped first class officer as a member of the regiment. It never had an American Army instructor come from outside to try and teach it anything, until about two months after the armistice had been signed, when, while waiting for a ship to take us home, . . . a young officer from a military school who had never heard a hostile shot, lectured the regiment upon . . . the open sight in battle.[57]

The 367th Infantry was organized at Camp Upton on Long Island on November 3, 1917, from drafted men. In the regiment's original force of 3,699, about 1,500 were from New York State. Nineteen soldiers were assigned to the 367th from the Army's 25th Infantry regiment, something the 15th New York never got. Although the 367th's colonel and eight other staff officers were white, the other 97 officers were black Americans, graduated from the Fort Des Moines Officer Training Camp. The 367th was assigned to the 92nd Division (Colored), AEF.[58]

The 367th's colonel was a West Point graduate and, a native of Louisiana, named James Moss who said of his command, "I am glad I am to command colored soldiers in this, my third campaign-in the greatest war the world has ever know." He even gave his regiment a nickname, "the Buffaloes" which became the symbol for the 92nd's shoulder patch.[59]

Colonel Moss was determined to put his regiment "on the map" and so spoke to the historic Union League of New York, which had helped recruit the 20th and 26th U.S.C.T. On March 23, 1918, the League gave the 367th its regimental flags. Moss also helped form the 367th Infantry Welfare League to help soldiers and their families. Former president Theodore Roosevelt became the honorary president of that organization, after speaking before the regiment on October 18, 1917.[60]

On February 22, 1918, it paraded with the 77th Division (the Statue of Liberty Division), something the 15th NY was never allowed to do with the 27th or 42nd Divisions. The 367th also received high praise from the local press. For example, the *New York American* stated the unit was "a serious, stolid, soldierly regiment to the last man." A white poet even wrote a lyric on the regiment, the last lines of which read, "A long way they have marched, . . . Men-citizens-at last."[61] Despite this bright picture, undertones of prejudice were directed toward the unit. For instance, Colonel Moss issued a directive that the black officers in his regiment would not have to require salutes from white soldiers.[62] Although this seems incomprehensible today, at that time, his directive was a reality.

When the 367th arrived in France on June 29, 1918, the men were ordered to stay out of French homes "under penalty of twenty-four hours on bread-and-water followed by an eighteen-mile hike with full pack . . ."[63] The 92nd Division's commander also strongly discouraged his soldiers from making friendly contacts with the locals. As Howard H. Long, a black officer who served with the 92nd Division, remembered, "Many of the field officers seemed far more concerned with reminding their Negro subordinates that they were Negroes than they were with having an effective unit that would perform well in combat . . . An infamous order from division headquarters . . . (even) made speaking to a French woman a disciplinary offense . . ."[64]

Once committed to combat, the 367th performed well. For instance, on November 10, 1918, in one of the last actions of the war, the regiment attacked at Pagny, opposite the Metz forts, in conjunction with two battalions of the French 56th Regiment. When the 56th ran into a murderous trap of barbed wire and was under withering machine gun fire, part of the 367th was sent into rescue the Frenchmen. As Scott stated, "Doubtless the entire force of the 56th would have been wiped out but for the timely rescue of the 367th. For this action the entire battalion was cited by the French commanding officer under whom the 56th was brigaded." Eventually, the whole 1st Battalion was awarded the Croix de Guerre.[65] At the time of this engagement, the battalion was commanded by Major Charles L. Appleton of New York "with company commanders and lieutenants, Negroes."[66]

Then there is the AEF's General Order #35, November 28, 1918, in which Private Bert Walker, 367th Infantry, was cited for meritorious conduct on November 9, 1918, in obtaining gas masks for his unit during a German gas attack. This same General Order also cited the 1st Battalion's Gas Officer, Lieutenant E.B.

William who, although himself already gassed, stayed at his post until all the shell holes were properly covered and his entire area free of gas.[67] According to Scott, the regiment's motto was "See it through," and from these examples, the officers and men lived up to that motto.

However, like the 369th no amounts of valor or awards could stop the discriminatory practices in the American armed forces. Tragically, when the 1st Battalion, 367th Regiment was ready to sail for home on the transport ship *Virginia*, which they had already coaled and had loaded with their personal gear, word came down from the ship's captain that no black troops had ever traveled on his ship and none ever would. To avoid a confrontation, the 367th was ordered not to sail on the ship and a white unit was boarded instead.[68]

The 92nd Division units were demobilized at Camp Meade and Camp Upton on March 6, 1919, and like the 369th, the 367th had a parade in the streets of New York City, in which they returned their regimental standards to the Union League. Like the 369th, the service of the 367th should have served as a shining example of what had been achieved by New York's black soldiers. Sadly, it was not to be, and what had been accomplished by the 367th, while in the 92nd Division, was besmirched and denigrated in the postwar years. As a result, another opportunity for ending the color line in New York State was lost.[69]

Finally, let the efforts of Cayuga County's African-Americans serve to illustrate what other New York State communities did during World War I.[70] When the draft was instituted for all men in New York State, in one of the first groups of black Cayugans called were Oscar Carter and Harry Dale from Auburn, along with Oscar Smith and J. McCully from Cayuga County. They were sent to Camp Upton, on Long Island, in August 1918. Whether these men served in the 367th, or in other units of the 92nd is still being researched.[71]

As local churches hung banners with stars to commemorate their members in the military, the Zion M.E. church, an African-American church on Parker Street in Auburn, dedicated a banner with three stars. The men so honored were parishioners William Newport, Phillip Gaskins, and Claude Freeman.[72] Although not living in Auburn at the time, Elmer Carter, a Harvard graduate and son of the Reverend Carter of the Zion M.E. Church, had already volunteered and joined the 325th Field Signal Battalion, 92nd Division, and served with distinction in France.[73]

From 1917 to 1919 New York State organized high school students into the Infantry Corps of Cadets for military training. In the case of the 2nd Battalion, 11th Regiment, Infantry Corps of Cadets, State of New York, a young black student from Auburn, Harry Jones, was in the 2nd Battalion. His school, the Auburn Academic High School, was integrated, and, as a result so was the 2nd Battalion of the 11th Regiment. His senior portrait may show him in this cadet uniform.[74] What all of these pieces of evidence suggest is that there might have been other such cadet units in the state that were integrated. As historian Laura Wilkes believed in 1919, researchers in our day may only be waiting to find documents in local archives and records on the service of black Americans.

When the 369th's band made a grand tour of New York State communities in April 1919, one of the places it gave a major concert was at a theater in Auburn. Henry Johnson to came to Auburn to formally lecture about his exploits in the 369th. Although evidence has not yet been found to document whether any black Cayugans served in the 369th, the appearance of the 369th's band, and of war hero Henry Johnson in Auburn points to the significance of the city and Cayuga County to African-Americans. The legacy of Harriet Tubman, William Seward, the Underground Railroad, and the record of Cayuga County's African-Americans in the Civil War, and their service in World War I was being honored by the 369th's band tour and Johnson's talk.[75]

Conclusion

What all of these pieces of evidence on the 15th Regiment, the 369th Infantry, the 367th Infantry, and the Cayuga County's black community show is the deep commitment of the African-Americans to the war effort. Yet, with victory over the Central Powers in 1918, the equality many in the black communities across New York State and the United States had hoped for did not come. Following the armistice, major racial violence broke out in America that would help dispel the desires of the war years for the advancement of African-Americans' civil rights. As one historian wrote about the years 1917 through 1919, "Black Americans had supported the war to the limit: ... (thousands) of their sons had gone into uniform, ... (many) had died in France; and this was their reward. They were bitter about it, they had a right to be bitter . . ."[76]

Indeed, the story of what did and did not take place from 1916 to 1919 can be labeled as another missed opportunity. The sacrifices and services of African-Americans during World War I should have cleansed America and New York State of their segregationist practices, but they had not. An incident at a soda fountain outside Camp Dix, New Jersey, in February 1919 dramatically illustrates what awaited many black veterans. After Corporals Lewis Jackson and Edward Buckley were refused service in such an establishment, they stated that the "colored soldier comes back from one of the world's greatest wars and finds that the money he has struggled for in this great war isn't any good at Mr. Alex Dubbell's half an half store."[77] The post war blues had arrived.

Chapter 5

The Postwar Blues, 1919–1939

The year 1919 was one that started with bright expectations for New York's black community but tragically evolved into an infamous summer of nationwide racial violence. On February 17, 1919, the 369th Infantry had left Camp Upton and made its famous parade before New York City crowds, estimated at more than one million spectators. The regimental band played many French military tunes that day, such as the stirring *Marche du Regiment de Sabre et Meuse* and the *Salute to the 85th*. This music was made even more appropriate as the drum line was using four captured German instruments to help sound the cadence.[1]

A New Yorker, who witnessed this monumental parade, wrote:

> I was strolling up Fifth Avenue on February 17, 1919, during lunchtime, with a lot of my buddies from school, when we heard the fanfare of bugles and the booming of drums . . . Even before the troops appeared, the sidewalks were jammed from building to curbs with spectators, for there was something odd about this parade right from the start. Most of the other parades came down Fifth Avenue—this was moving uptown!

We soon saw why. Back from the Rhine to get the applause of their city and of Harlem were the troops known in France as the 369th U.S. Infantry, but known in New York as the Harlem Hell Fighters.

Not till many years later would I understand the reason for the great impression of steel-helmeted power, those of us on the sidelines got that day. . . . Shoulder to shoulder, from curb to curb, they stretched in great massed squares [and] they tramped far up the Avenue in an endless mass of dark-skinned, grim-faced, heavy booted veterans of many a French battlefield.

Then we heard the music! Somewhere in the line of march was Jim Europe and his band that the French had heard before we ever did. . . .[2]

On February 18 the *New York Times* commented on the regimental parade that "New York's Negro soldiers, bringing with them from France one of the bravest records achieved by any organization in the war, marched amid waving flags . . ." Nicolas Murray Butler, president of Columbia University, praised the 369th and proclaimed, "When fighting was to be done, this regiment was there." *The Independent and Harper's Weekly* of March 1 felt that the 369th's band was one of the four best in the world, ranking with the British Grenadiers, the Garde Republicans, and the Royal Italian Band.[3]

A lead editorial in the *New York Tribune* of February 14 expressed words of hopeful insights on what the 369th's arrivals home should have meant:

The bas-relief of the Shaw Memorial became a living thing as the dusky heroes of the 15th cheered the Liberty statue and happily swarmed down the gangplank. Appropriately the arrival was on the birthday of "revered Lincoln," and never was the young and martyred idealist of Massachusetts filled with greater pride than swelled in Colonel Hayward as he talked of his men the best regiment, he said, with pardonable emphasis, "of all engaged in the great war."

These were men of the Champagne and the Argonne whose step was always forward; who held a trench ninety days without relief [and] who won 171 medals for conspicuous bravery. . . . First class fighting men. Hats off to them! The tribunal of grace does not regard skin color when assessing souls.

A large faith possesses the Negro. He has such confidence in justice, the flow of which he believes will yet soften hard hearts. We have a wonderful example of patience that defies discouragement; the "Soul of Black Folks!" When values are truly measured some things will be different in this country.[4]

These contemporary samplings make clear that a mood of optimism and pride cut across the city's ethnic groups. For many, it was hope that the service of the 369th would make a difference in the Empire State in civil rights for years to come. At least that was the mood in February 1919.

The spirit of that February was not just confined to New York City. In Buffalo similar parades to honor returning black veterans took place and when the 92nd Division landed in Hoboken in March 1919, New York City did not forget that command for another grand parade was held to honor these black servicemen. In Chicago the famous 370th Regiment (the old 8th Illinois, N.G., an all African-American regiment), paraded before jubilant crowds downtown and into the South Side. Yet, once the parades were over, black veterans, like their white counterparts, had to try and adjust to civilian life.[5] It soon became obvious, in the next few months, that the black veterans of the Great War had come home to a nation that, in many regions, still drew the color line as hard as it had ever been drawn before.

While the normalcy of civilian life tried to return to the nation, as black poet and writer James Weldon Johnson wrote, for African-Americans those summer days turned into "The Red Summer." Many cases of racial attacks, lynchings, mob violence, and major riots, especially in Washington and Chicago, broke out, many specifically directed toward black veterans. Seventy lynchings were recorded in that summer, with more than ten victims being ex-servicemen. These atrocities motivated President Wilson to speak out. The president condemned these horrendous acts, especially toward black veterans, since "our Negro troops are but just back from no little share in carrying our flag to victory."[6]

In New York State these racial attacks, along with the national resurgence of the Ku Klux Klan, were especially condemned by the black media. For instance in the *New York World*, an editorial writer commented on the issue of war, race, and nationalism with words of such poignancy that they bear careful reading:

> War has sinister markings of its own, won in all sufficiency. There is no room for the color line across its torrid front. Such is the thought that suggests itself afresh, for there have been other events calling to mind the gallantry of our colored troops. . . . The Negro has WON his decorations in France on "soldierly merit." He has WON at the same time by the manifestations of his courage, and his devotion and his loyalty, a more even chance in American life. And the victory should be made sure. . . . We do not intend now that we have served the Nation in every war of the Republic [but] to further accept the indignities heaped upon us as a race without a solemn protest to every sense of conscience and right in America.
>
> There is one thing this World War had done. It has lifted the Negro problem out of the provincialism of America into the circumspection of the civilized world. We purpose to carry our cause into the open forum of the world. We purpose to let the world know that the soldiers that brought glory to the American flag in the fields of France are denied common courtesies in too many cases when they return home. . . . We make this appeal to the world in no sense of disloyalty to our Nation. We do it because we are loyal. We will be heard. We will not be lynched and robbed and hedged about without a solemn protest. We do not plead for pity or sympathy. We want what we have earned by every rule of the game.[7]

However, the "rules of the game" had not been changed substantially by the dedicated service of black soldiers in World War I. In Washington, DC, a weakening Wilson Administration could not stop Congress from discouraging new black immigrants to the city, bills to segregate its streetcars were introduced, and even prestigious Howard University was threatened to have its appropriations cut. Outside government, the newly formed American Legion, at its 1919 national convention, set no nationwide standards for the admissions of black veterans. Instead, it permitted each state group to make its own rules that, generally, excluded black veterans from Legion posts. As a result, black veterans formed the League for Democracy to protest this side-stepping act of the American Legion and its Jim Crow attitudes. In 1924 the Lincoln Legion was formed, headed by George W. Lee and Charles P. Howard, graduates from the Fort Des Moines officers school, to help promote the record of black servicemen in World War I and to fight for the inclusion of African-Americans in the armed services and related organizations.[8]

Internationally the secret AEF Headquarters wartime memo, which had directed the French not to treat American black soldiers with more fairness and equality than they experienced at home, was exposed to the French Assembly. In July 1919 an indignant member of the French National Assembly, René' Boisneuf, read the AEF document to the French legislature. The French Assembly promptly passed a resolution condemning this AEF memo and expressed confidence that any infraction committed within French territory against black U.S. troops would be punished, no matter who the perpetrators or who the victims were.[9] Just to what extent this reaction exemplifies the values of liberty, equality, and fraternity or wounded French pride need not be discussed, but it is interesting to note that when the French war painting *Le Pantheon de la Guerre,* by Pierre Carrier-Belluse and Auguste Francois Gorguet, was unveiled, troops of all the Allied countries

were represented, except for one notable exception—the omission
of America's black soldiers.[10]

Controversy about the conduct of the 92nd Division had
surfaced while it was in France. In December 1918, Robert R.
Moton, Booker T. Washington's successor at Tuskegee, was sent
by President Wilson and Secretary of War Baker to investigate
rumors of high instances of rape among the men of the division.
The "fear" of massive raping of French women by black servicemen was proven unfounded, but it illustrates the temper of the
times by U.S. authorities.[11] Yet by war's end, the 92nd was being
praised by United States Secretary of War Baker for its actions in
the Meuse-Argonne offensive. In January 1919, General Pershing,
upon reviewing the 92nd, stated that he was "proud of the part

An unfinished sketch showing a variety of uniforms worn by the 369th Infantry,
National Guard, New York, ca. 1920–1925 by Raymond Johnson. (*Original in the
Anthony Gero collection*)

you played in the great conflict . . . you have only done what the American people expected you to do and you have measured up to every expectation of the Commander in Chief."[12]

But the controversy over the record of the 92nd Division, especially in combat, would not go away. Its commander, General Charles C. Ballou, said the division was "made the dumping ground for discards, both black and white. . . . In the last battle of the war, the Division did some very aggressive work, so far as the companies were concerned."[13] United States Army Historian Ulysses Lee wrote, "It was widely believed that the 92nd was established by Secretary of War Newton D. Baker and approved by President Wilson over the objections of the Army's General Staff," and by 1923 former black officers in the division had written many letters to black publications about the United States Army's undermining of the division and its record. As a result, black publications openly wondered about army policy in the past war and just how the army's new policy would treat black soldiers' combat abilities in the future.[14]

In 1925 General Robert L. Bullard, who had commanded the 2nd American Army, in which the 92nd Division had served in France, wrote that the "Negroes were a great disappointment" as combat troops.[15] His comments only added to the black communities feelings that a program was in place in the military to discredit the record of black soldiers in World War I. Finally, during the mid-1920s this negative attitude of the United States Army, as Lee wrote, "gained ascendancy over the optimistic reception of the first news from the front," which had so thrilled persons of color.[16] The prewar desire of African-Americans for better civil rights, fairly won on the fields of France, was being stymied and revised to fit patterns of segregationism that had existed before 1917.

Two other examples typify what transpired in this era. In 1924 a federal bureau decided to dedicate a plaque inscribed with the names of its servicemen killed during the war. Unfortunately, when unveiled, there were two tablets, one for the white soldiers and a separate one for the black servicemen. In 1930 Congress approved funding to send Gold Star mothers to Europe who wanted to visit their sons' graves. Thousands accepted, but when black mothers who wished to join were told they were to be assigned segregated quarters, trains, and hotels, several refused, saying they wished "to remain at home and retain our honor and self-respect." Others did go, but they went under segregated arrangements.[17]

In June 1925 letters began to appear in New York City papers defending the black soldier, especially the black veterans of New York. On June 12 Republican Congressman Hamilton Fish, formerly a major in the 369th, sent a letter to the *New York Tribune* defending the black soldier. On June 14, Captain L. Edward Shaw, also of the 369th, wrote the *Tribune*. In his correspondence, he stated that, "Since the war I have been answering constantly one question: 'What do you really think of the colored soldier?' My answer has always been, and still is, 'If there were another war tomorrow I should try to go with the colored troops . . .'"[18]

Captain Shaw, in that same letter, went on to note one of those events in history that gives us much insight into life, but, if not recorded by a contemporary, can be lost. Shaw stated that on June 14, 1925, at 3 o'clock, on Edgecomb Avenue and 136th Street, a square would be dedicated for a New York City born and raised soldier, Private Dorrance Brooks, 369th Infantry. Private Brooks had been killed in action in the Argonne-Meuse while leading forward remnants of the Third Machine Gun Company, after its four white officers, two black sergeants, and two corporals had been killed or wounded. Shaw felt that Dorrance's act of bravery from "a humble colored soldier from New York city honored the valor of the American colored soldier and stand as a permanent answer to all uniformed or prejudiced critics of the colored soldiers." Today, this historic square is maintained as part of the Greenstreet program in New York City.[19]

Despite the "The Red Summer" of 1919 and the designs of the Regular Army in the early 1920s, the 369th Infantry was still active in the Empire State. On September 6, 1924, the regiment was reorganized and federally recognized, with headquarters at New York City. Between 1924 and 1934 a regimental armory was built and expanded, and by War Department General Order 11, issued in 1924, the 369th was allowed the following decorations: "French Croix de Guerre with Silver Star, World War I, Streamer embroidered Meuse-Argone."[20] As a result, after 1924 the Empire State would not degenerate into its former exclusiveness and the 369th would be maintained in the military structure of the state.

As to the hopes for African-Americans' World War I service ending segregation and racial attacks in the United States, by 1930 not much had been accomplished. As Emmett Scott stated in 1933, "as one who recalls the assurances of 1917 and 1918 . . . I confess personally a deep sense of disappointment, of poignant pain that a great country in time of need should promise so much and afterwards perform so little."[21] During the last half of the 1920s and into the early 1930s, the 369th was, apparently, the only National Guard regiment of African-Americans allowed in the Empire State. Other segregated units were not created in places like Buffalo or Syracuse, which might have been able to maintain such units. The 369th's continuation did provide some military opportunities for black New Yorkers, especially when it went to the State Camp at Peekskill, but the regiment was watched carefully by Regular Army authorities, and its existence was tenuous. On one level, the Empire State was one of only two states, the other being Illinois, that had complete regimental-size African-American National Guard units in the period. More could have been accomplished on the national and state levels for African-Americans to join the national guard, but it was not to be.[22]

The United States Army and Navy still had some opportunities for the service of African-Americans, but their duties were mainly restricted to noncombat assignments. The downsizing of traditional African-American units, like the 9th and 10th Cavalry as a part of the Army's overall reduction, were loudly protested by the National Association for the Advancement of Colored People.[23] One might assume that black New Yorkers still served with the Regulars in the Army, but names of such individuals await research. Unfortunately, the United States Marine Corps did not allow African-Americans to enlisted prior to 1942.[24]

Although the Civilian Military Training Camps (CMTC), a federally sponsored organization formed in 1920, allowed, in some states, for segregated units, in New York State it was different.[25] Here in 1922, a black New Yorker Walter Bradley was given orders to report to the camp at Plattsburg. Upon his arrival, Bradley was told a mistake had been made and was sent home. In 1927 a high school student from New York City, Marsden V. Burnell, was barred from the CMTC. The *New York Times* carried an account of this in its April 6 edition, under the heading, "Army Bars Negro at Training Camp." In June 1931 Milton F. Quanders, an ROTC officer and a student at City College in New York City, was also denied acceptance in the CMTC program due to his ethnic background.[26]

The role of black Americans in the Civilian Conservation Corps (CCC), especially in New York, is of note, especially the views of Luther C. Wandall in 1935. Some reserve officers of African-American descent were also involved and one black company stationed at Elmira was officered by "Negro Reserve officers." However, the CCC, as well as Marcus Garvey's Universal Negro Improvement Association (UNIA), fall outside the scope of this book. Those interested in these groups, as well as the aid African-Americans sent to Ethiopia in 1936 or during the Spanish Civil War should look elsewhere for data on the involvement of black New Yorkers.[27]

The 1932 election of Franklin D. Roosevelt and his establishment in 1936 of the Federal Council on Negro Affairs, plus the informal network of black leaders he helped create known as the Black Brain Trust, seemed to offer some hope for the advancement of African-Americans.[28] In regard to the American military, it was still a major uphill battle as segregationists and racists in the federal bureaucracy resisted real reform.[29]

A small spark of change did happen within the 369th's command structure. In 1938 Benjamin O. Davis Sr., one of the few Regular Army's commissioned officers of African-American descent, was appointed as instructor and then as commander of the 369th Regiment. The appointment of Davis who, providentially, was to become the United States Army's first black general in World War II, was heralded by Governor Herbert H. Lehman in 1938. As the governor stated, "I believe that the state of New York and the 369th Regiment are indeed fortunate to obtain the services of such a well qualified commander."[30] The appointment of Colonel Davis, a highly qualified Regular Army officer, was, at the time, an achievement that many in the black and white communities took as a harbinger. Subsequent events from 1940 through 1950 would prove just how prophetic his appointment in 1938 was.

Colonel Davis moved his family to New York City and found his welcome there most cordial. In a June ceremony, with Governor Lehman, Albert Einstein, and thousands of spectators in attendance, Colonel Davis officially took command of the regiment. In the following days, he energetically promoted the 369th by making the social rounds in the city, even meeting with Mayor Fiorella LaGuardia, but Colonel Davis was no parade ground soldier. He also visited the armory regularly and helped train his command to the high standards of the United States Army. In 1940, with the assistance of Governor Lehman, Colonel Davis attempted to overcome the Regular Army attitude that the 369th could not handle the tasks of being converted to a modern antiaircraft unit. In early April, Colonel Davis went to Washington to try and convince

General George Marshall that the regiment could do the highly technical job of an AAA regiment. As a result of Colonel Davis's lobbying, the 369th was ordered to be converted to an AAA regiment. This achievement was much written about in the black press of the day as a sign of the black soldiers' abilities and equality in the expanding federal army of 1940.[31]

Lamentably, Colonel Davis four-year term as commander of the 369th expired, in part, due to his mandatory retirement age in 1941. As a result, he was reassigned, but as the events of 1940 and 1941 evolved, the career of this outstanding soldier was not to be ended, although his service with the 369th was.

Conclusion

What can be concluded about New York State's black soldiers from 1919 to 1939?

First, in the two decades following World War I, the Empire State did not go back to that long period of omission from 1866 to 1915 when there was no unit of black New Yorkers in its National Guard. The establishment of the 369th Infantry in 1924, as a part of the federal and state organization, was an achievement of no small measure, but compared to what should have been done, it was. Regrettably, neither New York State nor America was ready for substantial change in the patterns of segregation, especially in the military. Despite the proven record of black veterans in World War I, the status quo would be maintained in the Empire State's National Guard. Second, as the Great Depression came about, and as fascism and communism battled for the minds and souls of mankind, America would face serious threats. Today, in the twenty-first century, it is hard to realize that a millennium of evil could have resulted from those events. The defeat of the Axis Powers in 1945 was not inevitable. Fascism's victories from 1932 to 1941 were real and could have lead to a worldwide totalitarianism based upon racism, slavery, and war.

How in the 1940s would African-Americans across the United States, and specifically in New York, respond to these dangers, especially based on segregation in their homeland? In 1942, Joe Louis, who entered the American military in World War II, addressed this question allegedly stating, "There may be a whole lot wrong with America, but there's nothing that Hitler can fix."[32] A great crusade lay ahead for Americans of all ethnic backgrounds in those days. They, as a generation, inevitably faced this struggle with great personal courage, hardship, and, at times, personal sacrifice that resulted in the wounding and death of many who served. In the Empire State, African-Americans would become involved in these events to save America, as they had done in 1776, 1812, 1861, and 1917. What was at stake was too vital to be ignored. Fascism, as Joe Louis so aptly put it, was not a fix for America's problems, especially with regard to segregation inside and outside her military forces.

Chapter 6

The Great Crusade, 1940–1950

In the history of the United States from 1776 to 1940, Americans generally did not like to take on difficult tasks, unless seriously confronted with them. Such an instance came about in the 1930s and early 1940s, as fascism triumphantly marched across and took hold of Italy, Germany, and Japan. In the case of African-Americans, according to John Hope Franklin, "Negroes were among the earliest and most energetic Americans to condemn the fascism that was rising in Europe. They early learned to hate Nazism and its Aryan doctrines..." and, in the fateful year 1938, also condemned the takeover of Austria and the dismemberment of Czechoslovakia.[1] As the Nazi juggernaut overran Poland in September 1939, and conquered France in June 1940, it became obvious to many Americans that war would stretch forth its hands across the seas and menace all of the Americas.

Farseeing individuals within and outside the United States government saw the threats and attempted to prepare militarily for the upcoming battle, but it was a very near victory.[2] The United States Army had been reduced in size during the 1920s and early 1930s and black American involvement in it even more so. To give a brief example, in 1940 there were only five serving Regular Army officers of African-American descent in the United States Army. The Reserve Officers Training Corps senior programs at Howard University in Washington and Wilberforce University in Ohio were the main training grounds for black reserve officers and the only fully regimental size unit in the entire National Guard was the 369th Regiment of New York's National Guard.[3]

However, the United States Army's 1937 Plan and its 1940 Revision would help to change the downward trend in its size. Black Americans' involvement in the military's enlargement would be increased and would represent between 9 and 10 percent of the manpower pool available. In retrospect, the United States would benefit greatly by the service of African-American soldiers in the struggle against fascism that these plans created.[4]

Under the Selective Service Act of 1940, more than 3 million African-Americans were registered. By war's end, hundreds of thousands of black soldiers, sailors, airmen, marines, coast guardsmen, merchant mariners, and Civilian Air Patrol members would be on duty. African-American women would serve, too, in the WACS, the WAVES, the SPARS, and related units. In the vital civilian defense industries, black women served as well.[5]

Sometimes forgotten is Dr. Charles Drew's effort in 1940 on the blood plasma project in New York City for the Blood Transfusion Association. His work there would help save thousands of wounded soldiers lives during the war. After December 7, 1941, Drew headed the American Red Cross blood program, but eventually resigned over the United States military's policy of separating white blood from blood donated by African-Americans.[6]

The service of all these African-Americans was a remarkable effort especially since racial incidents at home, including lynchings, and segregationist policies overseas, within and outside of the military, were still evident during the war years. Just prior to the war, the loyalty of African-Americans was questioned by some within and outside the African-American communities, but as Representative Hamilton Fish of New York, a former officer in the 369th in World War I, declared in front of Congress on April 30, 1940, "99 1/2 percent of American Negroes are loyal American citizens."[7] How prophetic Representative Fish's words were, as subsequent events in World War II were to demonstrate.

At the federal level two major achievements would be accomplished for black Americans in the military. One was the nomination of Colonel Benjamin O. Davis Sr. as a general on October 25, 1940. As a result of his mandatory retirement due to age on July 31, 1941, Colonel Davis was reinstated as a general on August 1, 1941, a rank he held until 1948. Consequently, he became the first African-American general in the history of the United States Army. The other achievement was the appointment of William Hastie, Dean of the Howard University Law School as Civilian Aide on Negro Affairs to the Secretary of War. Hastie undertook his duties on November 1, 1940, and his appointment followed the precedent of Emmett J. Scott from World War I.[8]

The part that African-Americans played in the Allied victory in World War II involves so many hundreds of thousands that it is outside the parameters of *Black Soldiers of New York State* to do them complete justice. Just as a sample in the Army, the 92nd Infantry Division was reconstituted and was sent to Europe while the 93rd Infantry Division was sent to the Pacific; each had black New Yorkers in their formations. The famous 761st Tank Battalion had at least two New Yorkers, E. G. McConnell and Leonard "Smitty" Smith, both from Queens, in the battalion. The 99th Pursuit Squadron, part of the Tuskegee Airman, had many New Yorkers who served as pilots, several of whom were killed in training and by enemy action during the war. The 96th Engineers (Colored), who fought in the Pacific may also have had black New Yorkers among their ranks.[9]

For the sake of managing the story of New York's black soldiers, I shall take three case studies to document their record in defending the "four freedoms." The first deals with the 369th

A drawing of a sergeant, 15th Regiment, New York Guard, ca. 1943–1945 by Alan Archambault. *(Original in the Anthony Gero Collection)*

Regiment, now converted to a Coast Artillery Regiment in 1940. The second involves the 15th Regiment of the New York Guard, a home defense unit in New York State. The last case describes the efforts of Cayuga County's black community in World War II. From each, an understanding of the significant contributions made by New York's black soldiers can be glimpsed.

The 369th Regiment had been converted into a Coast Artillery (Antiaircraft) regiment before the USA's entry into the war. This 369th Coast Artillery (AA) should not be confused with the new 369th Infantry Regiment, of the new 93rd Infantry Division, which served in the Pacific. The 369th CA (AA), was the direct descendant of the old 15th New York formed in 1916.[10] Unfortunately, in World War II the 369th CA (AA) would see limited service in the Pacific area. The 369th CA (AA) was inducted into federal service on January 13, 1941, at New York and moved to Fort Ontario, Oswego, New York, on January 15. Photographs from the Fort Ontario Historic Site show the men training there, but they also show segregated USO dances at the post. The 369th received praise for its demeanor during its stay at Fort Ontario and actively participated in local community and sports events, despite some racial incidents.[11]

The regiment was transferred to Camp Edwards, Massachusetts on September 5, and moved to Los Angeles, California, Camp Stoneman, on May 5, 1942. The unit departed, via the port of San Francisco, on June 16, 1942, and arrived in Hawaii on June 21. Mainly confined to defenses in the Hawaiian Islands, it saw little action, and, in December 1943, the 1st and 2nd Battalions were redesignated as the 369th AAA and 870th Automatic Weapons Battalion, respectively. Cadres of men from the 369th AAA help to form three new battalions of AAA Gun Battalions at Camp Stewart, in Hinesville, Georgia, in that year as well. The 369th Regiment CA (AA) was inactivated on November 28 1944, its only honors awarded being the "Pacific Theater, without inscription." However, the 369th AAA Gun Battalion was sent to Okinawa in August 1945 and returned to the States in January 1946.[12]

As the record indicates, the 369th CA (AA) and the 369th AAA Gun Battalion were not allowed much of a role in combat operations during the war. The reasons why are hard to pin down exactly, but from a reading of Lee's *Special Study*, one can speculate that the regiment was hamstrung from the beginning, especially in regard to the number of officers assigned to it as per army regulations. Whether an official policy was in place to keep the 369th out of active combat zones is hard to document, but from looking at what was done to the 369th, to paraphrase a Shakespeare quote, "there is something rotten in Denmark." Neither the 369th CA (AA) nor the 369th AAA Gun Battalion achieved the high-profile combat record of their parent organization, the 369th Infantry of World War I.

After the 369th CA (AA) had become federalized, the question rose whether the Empire State would organize an African-American New York Guard unit to replace the 369th CA (AA). First, the New York Guard should not to be confused with the New York National Guard. The New York Guard (NYG) was a home-defense force used to protect vital sites in New York State and to act as a constabulary force, if needed, after the New York National Guard had been federalized. The New York Guard was formed in October 1940 by volunteers whose service "carried no remuneration and exacted a sacrifice of appreciable time and energy." By 1944, NYG strength was reported to be around 16,700 men.[13]

Other states, like Maryland in its State Defense Force, raised African-American home guard units, but would the Empire State?[14] New York State did in fact raise not one, but perhaps as many as three African-American NYG units between 1942 and 1946.[15] Several references to African-American NYG units appear in the the *New York Times* between 1940 and 1946. For example, the *New York Times* on October 23, 1942, page 23, column 7, had this small item:

> Guard To Have Negro Unit
> Governor Authorizes Battalion of Kings and Queen Recruits
> Special to *The New York Times*
> Albany, Oct 22—Governor Lehman has acceded to the request of a large group of citizens in Brooklyn and Queens and authorized the formation of a third separate battalion of the New York Guard, to be composed of Negroes and with headquarters in the State armory at 801 Dean Street, Brooklyn. The four companies will have twenty-one officers and 282 enlisted men.
>
> At present the Dean Street armory is used by Company L of the Fifth Regiment, which unit is to be transferred to the armory at 171 Clermont Street, where other units of the Fourth Regiment are stationed . . .

Several points are worth mentioning. First, the 4th Regiment and 5th Regiment were white units. Second, the new separate black battalion was to use the state armory on Dean Street for its drills making it easier for the unit to train. Lastly, it is interesting to observe that the newspaper mentions the pressure of citizens in Brooklyn and Queens as being a major factor in Governor Lehman's decision, but does not state by name, or group, who these citizens were.

On September 26, 1943, the *New York Times* stated, on page 50, column 1:

> Harlem Troops Training
> Two Guard Units Getting 10 Day Workout at Camp Smith
> Special to *The New York Times*
> Peekskill, N.Y.–Sept 25-
> Displacing the Twenty-first Regiment of Rochester and the Sixty-fifth Regiment of Buffalo, the Fifteenth Regiment and the Third Separate Battalion of Harlem, commanded by Col. W. Woodruff Chisum, arrived here Monday at Camp Smith for ten days of field training. The only Negro unit in the State Guard, the Fifteenth has in the field sixty-five officers and 600 enlisted men.
>
> Active training began Tuesday with all the officers and men taking the field for two days of rifle practice.
>
> Trained on both offensive and defensive tactics, the men are being prepared for mobilization and action in case of invasion. The handling of domestic uprisings and emergencies is also being taught in simulated battles. Night marches and the combat tactics are being carried out.
>
> Breaking camp on Wednesday the Fifteenth Regiment will conclude the season's field training of State Guard units here at Camp Smith.

It would appear that by this date in 1943 the 15th Regiment, NYG, had been organized and recruited, with close to seven hundred men in it. However, notice that the paper states that the regiment was the "only Negro unit in the State Guard." As a result, it seems that the NYG restricted the opportunity of New York State's black volunteers to join the Guard to the New York City region.[16]

Also, observe when these two African-American Guard units were allowed to exercise, after all the white units had received their summer training. It is quite obvious that the color line was to be maintained in training at Camp Smith by the NYG during the war years.

Finally, can one assume that the officers of the 15th Regiment and the 3rd Separate Battalion were African-Americans? Since this newspaper article provides a name, Colonel W. Woodruff Chisum, was he an African-American? It would seem reasonable to believe so, but research continues to document Colonel Chisum and his life.

On September 27, 1943, the *New York Times*, on page 21, column 1, provides some answers to the previously posed questions:

DEWEY REVIEWS STATE GUARDSM(sic)
Ceremony is Last of Season at Camp Smith, Where 1,000 Men are Inspected
TRAINING ENDS WEDNESDAY
15,000 Taught Offensive and Defensive Tactics, Handling of Domestic Uprisings
Special to *The N.Y. Times*
Peekskill, N.Y., Sept. 26-
Gov. Thomas E. Dewey reviewed this afternoon 1,000 State Guard members of Harlem and the Third Separate Battalion of Brooklyn in the last military ceremony of the training season at Camp Smith.

The training season will end when the two Negro units break camp on Wednesday after ten days in the field . . .

Motoring from his home in Pawling, the Governor, making his second visit to the camp this year, was welcomed by Maj. Gen. William Ottmann, commander of the Guard . . .

The Governor and his party made an inspection of the troops on foot, preceding the review. Accompanying him were Senator Joe R. Hanley, General Ottmann. . . . and Brig. Gen. Anson Goodyear, commander of the Second Brigade, of which the Fifteenth Regiment is a part.

An African-American Combat Volunteer, Europe, January 1945, a sketch by
Raymond Johnson. *(Original in the Anthony Gero Collection)*

The soldiers marched in review before some 2,000 persons,
most of them from New York City, with Col. W. Woodruff
Chisum leading the Fifteenth and Major Myles A. Paige leading
the Third. They are the commanders of the units.

Afterwards, addressing the soldiers and spectators over
a loudspeaker system, the Governor complimented the troops
on their showing, and, alluding to the Fifteenth said he was
'pleased to know that this organization in particular had such
a large turnout when called during the recent riot of hoodlums
in New York City.' This was a reference to the precautionary
mobilization of Guard organizations in Manhattan after the
outburst of looting in Harlem.

The Governor also spoke of the sacrifice the men had made in joining the Guard. He said the organization 'has its part in the war effort' and former members were 'doing better in the Army as result of training received in the Guard.'

After the ceremony the Governor was introduced to the officers at a reception in the Officers Club.

Several items are obvious. First, the 15th Regiment was from Harlem and commanded by Colonel Chisum, while the 3rd Separate Battalion was from Brooklyn, commanded by Major Paige. Second, the number of men in these two units was near or just above one thousand and shows a significant enrollment of African-Americans. Finally, since one of the purposes of the New York Guard was to prepare eligible men for Army service, the 15th Regiment was helping to do that. As mentioned by the governor, former members of the 15th NYG were "doing better in the Army as a result of training received in the Guard."

For Governor Dewey, who had been elected in 1942, to appear at Camp Smith in September of 1943 and to praise these African-American units shows his appreciation of these officers' and men's efforts. The fact that two thousand residents of New York City came to watch this ceremony also speaks volumes of its importance for black New Yorkers. Since the governor makes mention of the Harlem disturbances and of these units' role, the constabulary nature of the New York Guard was demonstrated, especially in those troubled days of 1943.[17]

On September 30, the *New York Times*, on page 24, column 3, wrote that "more than 1,700 officers and men received a ten-day period of instruction" from the 15th Regiment and Third Separate Battalion. What this small item suggests is that the enrollment in these units was more than had been inferred in the September 27 article. Whatever the real number was, it was well over one thousand men and shows a substantial voluntary enrollment by African-Americans in the NYG whose strength, as previously stated in 1944, was just over sixteen thousand men.

During 1944 and 1945, the *New York Times* reported minor blurbs on these two units like annual indoor inspections and summer training at Camp Smith. An interesting article about the entire Guard appeared in August 1944 that "Each regiment now has a machine gun platoon equipped with the Browning water cooled .30 caliber gun of the Army." From this I assume the 15th Regiment was equipped with a machine gun platoon as well.[18]

On March 19, 1946, a small *New York Times* article, on page 18, column 2, points out several important facts about the New York Guard's discriminatory policies:

> Segregation Protested
> Separation of Negro Units in State Guard Called "Disgraceful"
> The National Association for the Advancement of Colored People, Wilkie Memorial Building, 20 West Fortieth Street, made public yesterday a resolution sent to Brig. Gen. Ames T. Brown, State Adjutant General, condemning "the segregation policy" of the New York State Guard.
>
> The association declared that "the public policy of this most socially progressive State" in the past has been "to strike out against every indication of discrimination or segregation based solely upon a citizen's race, creed, color or national origin." To continue to require separate Negro units in the State Guard "is illogical, unwarranted, and disgraceful," the statement said.
>
> Besides objecting to "over-all segregation" the association took the position that "hardship is imposed upon the individual Negro who wants to enlist in a community where there is no separate unit.

This article answers the question as to why African-American units were not raised in the upstate areas since the Guard was limiting enrollment of black New Yorkers to the New York City area. The NAACP in this 1946 article was protesting not only the segregationist policies of the New York Guard, but the Guard's policy to limit African-American participation to the immediate New York City area. Additionally, the NAACP was calling for integration of the Guard in those areas of the state where black

New Yorkers may have wanted to join a Guard unit, but where local black population size could not support segregated units. The NAACP's protest reflects a dramatic effort to integrate the Guard in 1946, but it seems to have generally failed, but then again, maybe it didn't. Other 1946 newspaper items hint at a possible racial experimentation in the NYG. For example, on September 22, 1946, in the *New York Times*, on page 55, this account appeared:

> Negro Units Earn Praise At Smith
> State Guard Troops in Training Rated Among Best-Break Camp Wednesday
> Special to *The New York Times*
> Peekskill, N.Y., Sept. 21-Rated as among the best disciplined units of the State Guard, the Negro troops of the Fifteenth Regiment of Harlem, commanded by Col. W. Woodruff Chisum, the Third Separate Battalion of Brooklyn, led by Major Myers A. Paige, and the First Platoon of Company B of the First Quartermaster Battalion of Manhattan, on a twelve-day training tour here at Camp Smith are hard at work becoming familiar with modern combat tactics.
> With eighty-four officers and 829 men the Fifteenth Regiment has a full complement in the field as has the Third Infantry Battalion with twenty-seven officers and 393 men. These coupled with the troops of Company B places more than 1,400 in the field.
> To many of the officers and men, whose ages range from 17 to 55 years, the training schedule is anything but new, as about 40 per cent of those in training have had previous service either in the United States Army or the National Guard. Nearly all senior officers and many non-commission officers were in service during the first or second World War . . .[19]

This article gives an idea of the strength of these units, close to 1,400 men, and shows much about their composition and readiness. It indicates, too, that many of the senior noncommissioned officers had served in the World War I and World War II, which would add to these units' overall reliability and pride.

A mystery remains, however. Was the 1st Platoon of Company B, 1st Quartermaster (QM) Battalion, NYG, an African-American platoon, while the rest of the Company B was "white?"[20] I believe this was the case since the 1st Platoon of Company B was training with the 15th Regiment and 3rd Separate Battalion at Camp Smith in September 1946.

This *New York Times* article raises several other questions. First, was this 1st QM Depot Company expanded to a battalion by 1946? If this was so, was the unit now called the First Quartermaster Battalion? Again, I believe the answer is yes, but, unfortunately, I could find no other references in the *New York Times Index* on this particular QM Battalion of the NYG. If these clues to the composition of the 1st Platoon of Company B are correct, it shows an interesting development in the New York Guard, before President Truman ended military segregation in the Regular Army in 1948. Additionally, in late 1944 and early 1945, the United States Army had experimented with segregated platoons in white infantry and armored divisions in Europe. One black New Yorker who served in such a platoon was Bruce M. Wright, assigned to the 26th Regiment, 1st Infantry Division.[21] Perhaps, back in New York State in 1946, the NYG was hesitantly doing the same, but since the NYG was demobilized in 1949, data on this 1st Platoon, Company B, QM Battalion is hard to find. Research continues on the New York Guard's possible experimentation with integration, but much documentation on NYG units during World War II has been lost or destroyed.[22]

As a final example of what was happening from 1940 to 1945, let me return to Cayuga County. Hundreds of Cayugans of all ethnic backgrounds served in the war, from Pearl Harbor to the bloody beaches of Normandy, in the skies over Europe and Japan, in the islands of the Pacific, and in the final victory ceremony aboard the U.S.S. *Missouri*.[23] The record of one African-American family, from the city of Auburn, speaks volumes for all those Americans who participated in this grand crusade of World War II. Mr. and Mrs.

Leroy Johnson of 49 Fitch Avenue had four sons in the military at one time: George, Kenneth, Chauncey, and Ernest. George was wounded in Italy while serving with the 317th Medical Battalion of the 92nd Division, while Kenneth was with the 350th Field Artillery in Germany. The other two sons were also called up during the war, and research continues on their records.

Many other Cayugans of African-American descent served too. The Hardy family of Auburn had two sons in the military during the war. Willard Hardy was accepted for the 99th Pursuit Squadron, while his brother, Charles Hardy, was in the army. A January 16, 1942, newspaper item, in the *Citizen-Advertiser* of Auburn, helps to document what Willard Hardy was about to undertake:

> Willard Hardy Enrolled as Flying Cadet
> Willard Hardy, 23, son of Mrs. Ethel D. Hardy of 72 Chapman Avenue, has finally obtained his long cherished wish-to join the Flying Cadets of the United States Army. Announcement has come that he has passed examination with a high rating and will be enlisted within the near future in the 99th Pursuit Squadron, to be composed of colored cadets. The squadron is in training at Tuskegee, Ala.
>
> Hardy is believed to have the distinction of being the first colored man in this part of the state to qualify for the Flying Cadets. He will undergo a minor operation at his own expense before entering the service. He was graduated from Auburn Senior High School in 1936 and has taken an active part in the Young People's circle of Thompson Memorial Church.
>
> In an examination held in Syracuse, under the direction of the United States Army officers, Hardy got a mark of 93. He recently took a refresher course in mathematics and other required subjects in order to pass the requirements for the Air Corps.[24]

Last, there was the sacrifice of PFC Charles Philip Johnson, age 29, killed in France in January of 1945, reportedly serving with the 118th Reinforcement Detachment. At the time of his death, PFC Johnson left a wife and four children, plus several brothers and sisters, at home. Whether or not PFC Johnson was a part of those African-American replacement platoons in the European Theater of Operations (ETO) is still being researched, but his sacrifice was huge, nonetheless. Recently, he was honored in ceremonies in Auburn in November 2004 that paid homage to his memory and sacrifice.[25]

For a small upstate county, Cayuga County's African-American residents responded well to their nation's call. A photograph of fifteen of these veterans, after their return home, taken at a reception at the Thompson Memorial Church in Auburn, was displayed at the Cayuga Museum of History and Art in 2004. The faces of these men, as captured in the image, show their youth, their joy at being home, and their pride of service. Some of the determination they carried with them from their military service is evident, too.

Conclusion

What could the black veteran in America, and in particular New York State, look forward to now that the war against fascism was over? As national and state events were to prove, it would not be more of the same acceptance of segregationist policies in the military or in civilian life. For example, New York had taken steps in 1945 to prohibit employment discrimination. Also in that year, Branch Rickey of the Brooklyn Dodgers met with Jackie Robinson, a veteran of World War II, to discuss the possibility of Robinson's becoming the first black player in the white professional leagues since 1889 when major league baseball had been integrated.[26]

In 1948, President Harry Truman's Executive Order 9981 was issued that led to the integration of the armed forces. Many forget, in the scope of our history, that this military integration was well ahead of civilian acceptance of the same practice.

Finally, in 1954 the United States Supreme Court made its historic ruling that began to transform the traditional segregationist status of America.[27] As the events of the late 1950s and early 1960s proceeded, the promise and hope expressed in 1776, which should have been achieved by black soldiers Civil War service in preserving the Union, were being legislatively and judicially addressed head on. It had been a long struggle, and it continues today, but for the black soldiers from New York State, the old color line, the old omissions, the old entrenchments, would be put to ground in the last half of the twentieth century.

One of those who helped to end the military attitudes in a truly gallant way was PFC William Thompson. Raised in Brooklyn, PFC Thompson was presented, posthumously, the Congressional Medal of Honor for his heroism during the Korean War. Private Thompson, while serving with Company M, 24th United States Infantry Regiment, made the consummate sacrifice on August 2, 1950, during heavy fighting against enemy forces. His medal certificate reads: "by conspicuous gallantry and intrepidity above and beyond the call of duty in action against the enemy. While his platoon was reorganizing under cover of darkness, fanatical enemy forces in overwhelming strength launched a surprise attack . . . Pfc. Thompson set up his machine gun in the path of the onslaught and swept the enemy with withering fire . . . thus permitting the remainder of his platoon to withdraw. . . . Although hit repeatedly by grenade fragments and small-arms fire, he resisted all efforts of his comrades to induce him to withdraw, steadfastly remained at his machine gun and continued to deliver deadly, accurate fire until mortally wounded by an enemy grenade. Pfc. Thompson's dauntless courage and gallant self-sacrifice reflect the highest credit on himself and uphold the esteemed traditions of military service."[28]

Since no African-American soldier had been decorated with the Medal of Honor during World War I or World War II, despite deeds by several above and beyond the line of duty, Private Thompson's medal merits the attention of all New Yorkers.[29] Yet, one wonders how many New Yorkers today know of his valor in the Korean War and of his supreme sacrifice for his platoon?

Chapter 7

What the Record Proves

Solon, an ancient Roman, wrote, "Good things are hard," and thus it was for African-American soldiers in the Empire State during their two hundred years of service from 1750 to 1950. Not only did they have to face a soldier's life and risks, but these black servicemen had to confront discrimination at home and overseas. New York State's motto is the Latin word *excelsior*, or "ever upward." If one looks at the overall progress of New York's black soldiers, it has been an ever upward movement. Yet, the achievement of integration was a long time in coming and in the Empire State many opportunities had been squandered before 1950.[1]

Black Soldiers of New York State has documented the progress of New York's black soldier as one of fits and starts. In the French and Indian War, although the number of African-Americans in New York's colonial militia was small, they were there nonetheless. During the Revolutionary War, black New Yorkers, both free and slave, served honorably. These men helped fortify New York City, fought in the continental and militia forces, and stayed the course for American independence. There were attempts to alter life in the Empire State after 1783, but the issue of slavery, that "peculiar institution" as one historian labeled it, and of segregationism had too strong a hold. Not until 1817 was slavery legislated to end by 1827 in New York.

In the War of 1812, men of African descent living in New York served in privateer vessels commissioned by the state, worked on New York City's defenses, and were on the northern frontier with Canada. In the Regular Army and Navy of the United States, their place is a matter of record. Their service in the War of 1812 should not be among the missing pages of that conflict. It is not political correctness to say that New York State, and the nation, benefited from these black soldiers, sailors, and volunteers. The contribution of New York's African-American servicemen had already been forgotten once, between 1816 and 1859, and must not be repeated in our day. Fairness to the record demands that these men be remembered in the annals of the Empire State's military history.

As presented in *Black Soldiers of New York State*, the American Civil War gave dramatic proof of the importance of the Empire State's black soldiers. With more than four thousand men from New York of African-American descent serving in volunteer regiments, such as the 54th Massachusetts Volunteer Infantry, the 20th, 26th, and 31st United States Colored Troops, it is not dramatic license to state, when coupled with the black men from Massachusetts or Pennsylvania or other states, that these soldiers help save the Union. The black volunteers of 1863 to 1865, along with their white counterparts from all across the United States, washed away with their service the shame of American slavery. The evidence is conspicuous on this point.

The tragedy of the years after the Civil War years was that segregation's stigma was not ended. New York was not immune from these practices, as was seen in the period of the great omission in its military forces. As the record indicates, no African-American soldiers were allowed in the National Guard from the Empire State between 1866 and 1915.

With the coming of World War I, a largely unspoken promise circulated in the African-American communities. What was it? That America would, by the courageous wartime service of African-Americans, finally establish equal justice and end the Jim Crow mentality. That was the expectation of the majority in the African-American communities in 1917 and 1918. Did it happen? It should have. Had not the combat record of the old 15th Regiment, New York, National Guard, which became the famous 369th United States Infantry that served in France, demonstrated their bravery? Had not the fighting achievements of the 367th Infantry, 92nd Division, shown that, too? Had not thousands of African-Americans from the Empire State gone into uniform, with hundreds dying in France? Were these not significant evidence of duty, honor, and country?

I believe they were, which is why the segregationists, within and outside of the United States Army, tried so hard to denigrate the black combat soldiers' achievements. Even during the war, as witnessed by the controversy over the 92nd Division's abilities, attacks began to modify and to slant the record of African-American combat soldiers. One of the fuels for "The Red Summer" of 1919 was the sight of thousands of returning black veterans, many of whom would not tolerate the old color line. That was why more than ten veterans were lynched in 1919, acts even President Wilson spoke out against, but that Congress made no provisions to make illegal and that persisted even into World War II.

From 1920 to 1936, the actions of the United States Army demonstrated clearly the undercurrent of segregationism and Jim Crow that wished to relegate the black soldier to service troops. This attitude was still prevalent in 1940. As Dean Hastie so aptly stated: "We will be American ditchdiggers. We will be American aviators. We will be anything that any other American should be in the whole program of national defense. But we won't be black auxiliaries."[2] How ironic it was that it took the major threat of fascism in the 1930s and early 1940s to force Americans to confront their apartheid system, yet that is what happened. Once again, as in 1776, 1812, 1861, and 1917, African-Americans, many from New

York State, did their duty overseas and on the home front. These men and women served honorably, as did millions of their white counterparts, such as my father, Samuel Gero (Grigolio), who was in combat with the 78th Infantry Division in Europe.

When these veterans came home, they wanted to return to lives of normalcy but, this time for the African-American veterans there was to be a difference. During the war years from 1939 to 1945, black soldiers and civilians, with the assistance of organizations like the NAACP, kept up the pressure for societal changes. Once the final Allied victories came against Nazi Germany and Imperial Japan, America would not be allowed to revert back to the old ways of segregation. As John Hope Franklin so eloquently stated:

> Among the numerous adjustments the American people had to make at the end of World War II was an adaptation to a new position of the Negro in the United States. This new status arose not merely because a substantial portion of the gains made during the war were retained but also because of an intensification of the drive . . . to complete equality for the Negro. . . . Negro organizations, notably the N.A.A.C.P., began to press more vigorously for full equality. . . . The courts, chiefly, but not exclusively the federal ones, showed a disposition to take cognizance of racial questions. . . . The executive branch of the federal government itself, moreover, sensitive both to domestic and foreign pressures, exerted considerable influence in eradicating the gap between creed and practice in American democracy. The interaction of these forces created a better place for the Negro Americans as the nation moved into the second half of the twentieth century.[3]

As presented in *Black Soldiers of New York State*, black soldiers faced the dual challenges of war and race but, remarkably, they did so with determination and courage. Courage is a word often misused today, but courage it was, and for that we should all be humbled.

In May 1919 W.E.B. Dubois penned these lines:

We return
We return from fighting
We return fighting.
Make way for Democracy! We saved it in
France and by the Great Jehovah, we will
save it in the United States of America
or know the reason why.[4]

His call for an American society, based on equality, did not happen then, but in 1948, a man of great courage himself, a veteran of World War I, issued a presidential executive order that helped to bring down the wall of military segregation. From the dust of that facade's fracturing, a precedent was established well in advance of the general civilian society.

The Roman historian Tacitus wrote, "The principal office of history I take to be this: to prevent virtuous actions from being forgotten, and that evil words and deeds should fear an infamous reputation with posterity."[5] What *Black Soldiers of New York State* has demonstrated are the many virtuous actions of New York's black soldiers from 1750 to 1950. The evidence is compelling on their service. It would be wicked not to recall their deeds. Such an action on our part might, as Tacitus suggested, be labeled infamous to our posterity.

According to Martin Luther King Jr., "If a man hasn't discovered something he would die for, he isn't fit to live."[6] From 1750 to 1950, the African-American soldiers from New York State found that something, and it was called equality. Theirs was a proud legacy, bequeathed to all Americans as a part of our common heritage, and should be passed on to all our children. In our remembrance of these soldiers services and sacrifices lies our state's and nation's dreams, so poignantly spoken about in 1963 on the mall in Washington, DC, on that bright day.

Notes

Preface

1. Mary T. Higgins, *Thomas Wentworth Higginson: The Story of His Life* (Boston: Houghton and Mifflin and Company, 1914), 206.

2. Arthur Barbeau and Florette Henri, *The Unknown Soldier: Black American Troops in World War 1* (Philadelphia: Temple University Press, 1974), xii. Douglass' statement is well-known by historians, but not by the general public. In their excellent book, Barbeau and Henri use it to document what should have been known prior to World War 1, but sadly had been forgotten.

Chapter 1

1. Laura E. Wilkes, *Missing Pages in American History: Revealing The Services Of Negroes In The Early Wars In The United States Of America, 1641–1815*, Press of R.L. Pendelton, Washington, DC 1919, 5. In her bibliography on New York, Wilkes lists the following sources for her observations of colonial New York: "1. *Field Book of the American Revolution*, Lossing; 2. *Our Country*, Lossing; *American Archives, 5th Series, Vol. 1-Force*; *New York in the Revolution*, Fernow; 5. *Camp Fires of Afro-Americans*, Wilson; 6. *American Patriots of the Revolution*, Nell,W.C." Those

familiar with these sources will note that Wilkes' research, for the time period, was very sound indeed.

    2. The reason for this choice is twofold: first, many historians consider the French and Indian War, or the Seven Years War, as the first world war among the European powers who used substantial numbers of men of African descent in the colonies for defense. Second, since my area of interest and research begins around the mid-eighteenth century, this war seemed an obvious point to begin. For an example of the Dutch use of slaves as soldiers in the 1600s consult A. Judd Northrup, "Slavery in New York," *State Library Bulletin, History No. 4, May 1900,* University of the State of New York, Albany, 1900, 246–253.

    3. The Muster Rolls for New York's colonial militia can be found in Edward F. DeLancey (ed.), *Muster Rolls of New York Provincial Troops, 1755–1764,* published originally in 1891, hereafter cited as *Muster Rolls.* By English tradition, only freemen were libel for military service in the militia. One can assume that the individuals designated as "Free Negro" or "Mulatto," with a first and last name, were indeed free and performing their duties as members of colonial New York. The rolls also contain the designation of "Indian" as well. For example, on 80–83, several men who passed muster in the County of West Chester, on 20 April, 1758, are listed as Indians, such as an Abraham Mompay, listed in Captain Jona Fowler's company.

    4. *Muster Rolls,* for the year 1758, had references on 60–61, 72–73, 80–81, 88, 116–117, 126–127, 130–131, 156–157 and 198–199 of individuals listed as Negro, Free Negro, and Mulatto, with different spellings of that word, for various companies in the aforementioned New York counties. Again, the designation "Free Negro" speaks for itself, while a man labeled a Mulatto, but with first and last name, could be assumed to be free. As for those men listed with only one name, as in Cuff, their status is open to debate as masters could send their slaves to fofill the owner's military duty.

    5. *Muster Rolls,* 126–127. Other names listed were "Joseph Nickles, Molata; Soloman, Molatto; Cuff, Mollato;" see also 80–81.

    6. *Muster Rolls,* 198 and 240–241. It must be noted that the spelling of Kellis had changed to "Killis, Mullato: Age 19, b Brook Have Suffolk County, Lab." Since spelling was not a forte of the eighteenth century, that

could account for the difference. The 1760 man's age and birth place are consistent with the one listed for the 1759 muster and one could assume it is the same individual. In 1760 the man's company was listed as under Captain Josiah Smith's, but company officers could change, which may account for this discrepancy.

7. For a history of the 3rd Battalion and its uniforms see: Gary Zaboly and John R. Elting's "3rd New York Battalion, 1758," Plate No. 541 in the *Military Collector and Historian*, Vol. XXXI, No. 2, Summer 1983, 79, as published by the Company of Military Historians in their uniform series entitled: *Military Uniforms in America*. Although Zaboly and Elting do not show any African-Americans in the 3rd Battalion, other battalions may have had free Negroes and mulattos in them, see *Muster Rolls*, 88 for Captain John Peter Smith's Company of New York Troops under the command of Colonel DeLancey for 1758; also a Capt. John VanVeghten's Company of the 2nd NY Regiment for 18 May 1761 lists a "Collivan Ludlow, Negro: Age 27b Long Island" on the rolls, *Muster Rolls*, 364–365.

8. *Wilkes*, 17–21. For an excellent study of African-Americans in the Revolutionary War period, consult Benjamin Quarles, *The Negro in the American Revolution*, published for the Institute of Early American History and Culture at Williamsburg, Virginia, by the University of North Carolina Press, Chapel Hill, 1961; John Hope Franklin, *From Slavery to Freedom: A History of Negro Americans*, Alfred A. Knopf, Inc., 1947, 1956, has data on the role of blacks in the French and Indian War. As an example of localized studies, which include data on the French and Indian War see: Fitzhugh McMaster, *Soldiers and Uniforms: South Carolina Military Affairs, 1670–1775*, Tricentennial Booklet Number 10, University of South Carolina Press, Columbia, SC, 1971 for observations on black soldiers there.

9. For examples of colonial French and Spanish use of black soldiers see: Jack D.L. Holmes, *Honor and Fidelity: The Louisiana Infantry Regiment and the Louisiana Militia Companies, 1766–1821*, Louisiana Collection Series of Books and Documents On Colonial Louisiana, Birmingham, 1965; Roland C. McConnell, *Negro Troops of Antebellum Louisiana: A History of the Battalion of Free Men of Color*, Louisiana State University Press, Baton Rouge, 1968.

10. *Wilkes*, 21.

11. *Quarles*, 8 where he quotes British General Edward Braddock, writing from Williamsburg, Virginia in 1755, "There are here numbers of mulattos and free Negroes of whom I shall make bat men, whom the province are to furnish with pay and frocks." Quarles lists this quote as being taken from Stanley Pargellis (editor) *Military Affairs in North America, 1748–1765*, New York, 1936, the standard reference work on British military operations in North America. A "bat man" is the British military term for an officer's servant. In the eighteenth century these "bat men" were usually enrolled on the regimental lists of the unit their officer was serving with.

12. Researchers continue to find evidence on Roger's Rangers that might prove that black men were in it; for example see: Timothy J. Todish and Gary S. Zaboly, *The Annotated and Illustrated Journals of Major Robert Rogers*, Purple Mountain Press, LTD, Fleischmanns, New York, 2002.

13. *Quarles* 83–93 and 152–156 devotes extensive pages to black seaman and pilots.

14. See Quarles and Franklin's works. For a short, but very interesting view, using contemporary documents and portraits, consult: Lisa W. Strick, *The Black Presence in the Era of the American Revolution, 1770–1800*, Smithsonian Institution, Washington, DC, 1973. For examples of localized studies, David O. White, *Connecticut's Black Soldiers, 1775–1783*, published by the Pequot Press, Chester, Connecticut, 1973 and Jeffrey J. Crow, *The Black Experience in Revolutionary North Carolina*, Division North Carolina Archives and History, 1977 are very good. For an early study of black men in the Revolution, W.B. Hartgrove's "The Negro Soldier in the American Revolution," *Journal of Negro History, Volume 1, #2, April 1916,* which predates Wilkes' work. One wonders if Wilkes used Hartgrove for her history, but since she did not list his work in her bibliography, my question is moot. William C. Nell's *The Colored Patriots of the American Revolution*, R.F. Wallicut, Boston, 1855, has accounts on black soldiers. Note, Wilkes used Nell as one of her sources in 1919.

15. Peter F. Copeland and James P. Simpson, "11th New Hampshire Provincial Regiment, 1774–1775," as reproduced in *Military Uniforms in America: The Era of the American Revolution, 1755–1795*, from the Series produced by the Company of Military Historians, edited by John R.

Elting, Presidio Press, 1974, 42–43, hereafter *The Era of the American Revolution*.

16. *Quarles*, 17, footnote 53, as quoted in *The Colonial Laws of New York: 1664–to the Revolution*, 5 Vols. (Albany, 1894–1896), V, 738. For interesting segments on black New Yorkers 1764–1775 consult: A.J. Williams-Myers: *Long Hammering: Essays on the Forging of an African American Presence in the Hudson River Valley to the Early Twentieth Century*, Africa World Press, Inc., Trenton, NJ, 1994.

17. Robert K. Wright Jr., *Army Lineage Series: The Continental Army*, Center of Military History, United States Army, Washington, DC, 1983, 55, hereafter *Army Lineage*. Note when the ban on reenlisting was lifted which suggests that, prior to January 1776, Free Negroes were serving.

18. *Quarles*, 52–60.

19. *Wilkes*, 40. For more information on the 2nd NY Regiment see *Army Lineage*, 248–249.

20. *Quarles*, 59. As of yet, I have found no other data on Field's service, nor the name of the slave sent by Belknap to Fort Montgomery.

21. *Quarles*, 77, shows others examples of black men as drummers; see also a list of officers and men of the 22d Beat, Capt. Benjamin Egbert's company, 2nd Militia Regiment where Frederick Bassett's Tom is listed as a drummer, found in *Calendar of Historical Manuscripts Relating to the War of the Revolution*, Volume I, Albany, 1868, 267, supplied by Eric Manders. Eleven "Negroes Belonging to the 22d Beat at Work" are also listed in this company; Ira Berlin and Leslie M. Harris (editors) *Slavery In New York*, published in conjunction with the New York Historical Society, New York: The New Press, 2005, "Chapter 3–Liberty and Constraint: The Limits of Revolution," by Graham Russell and Gao Hodges, 97.

22. *Quarles*, 98. His source was the *American Archives, 4th Series*, V, 218–219.

23. *Wilkes*, 38–39; *Quarles*, 146.

24. *Wilkes*, 39–40; *Quarles*, 70. Wilkes quotes this act more extensively than does Quarles, but each gives evidence that, if a slave completed his three year term, freedom was the reward.

25. As of yet, I have seen no data on whether these two regiments were actually raised and fielded.

26. For recent research on the Rhode Island Regiment's uniforms especially the ones worn on this brutal campaign up to Oswego, see Alan Archambault and Marko Zlatich, *"Rhode Island Regiment, 1781–1783, Plate No. 559,"* in *Military Uniforms in America*, as published by the Company of Military Historians. Quarles devotes much to the Rhode Island Regiment, but not to its uniforms; see also *Army Lineage* for historical details on the entire service record of the Rhode Island Regiment; for a brief view of Bakeman's service consult Lillian S. Williams, Amybeth Gregory, Hadley Kruczek-Aaron's essay on "African Americans" in Peter Eisenstadt, Editor in Chief, *The Encyclopedia of New York*, Syracuse University Press, 2005, 1.

27. See Holmes for Spanish and French usage; Lt. Charles M. Lefferts, *Uniforms of the American, British, French and German Armies in the War of the American Revolution*, originally published c. 1926, but reprinted by We. Inc., Old Greenwich, CT has data on German troops using black musicians. In *The Era of the American Revolution* researchers have discovered much on the use of blacks among the Germanic troops while in North America. Some of these black soldiers returned to Europe with their units after the war. Quarles also devotes observations on the use of escaped slaves in the British, Loyalist, and Germanic forces during the war; Gary S. Zaboly, "Occupied New York Extracts on the Uniforms, Arms, and Equipment of the British Army and Navy from Royalist Newspapers, 1776–1783," *Military Collector and Historian*, Vol. 56, No. 3, Fall 2004, 188.

28. E. Cruikshank's *Butler's Rangers: The Revolutionary Period*, Lundy's Lane Historical Society, 1893, 116 lists a "Baker, Jack (blackman) on 117, a "Martin, Peter (negro)" and "Parepoint, Richard (negro)," 120; *Berlin and Harris*, "Chapter 3–Liberty and Constraint: The Limits of Revolution," by Graham Russell and Gao Hodges, 99–100. One of the more interesting black men named Benjamin Whitecuff, a freeman born in New York, is listed in Russell and Hodges' essay.

29. Erastus C. Knight, Comptroller, and edited by Frederic G. Mather, *New York in the Revolution as Colony and State: Supplement*, Oliver A. Quayle, Albany, NY, 1901, 120. Whether these two men are one in the same is, at present, unclear. Research continues to see if they did, in fact, settle on their land grants.

30. Professor Quarles devotes his whole Chapter X to this issue.

31. Raymond W. Logan, "The Negro in the Quazi War 1798–1800," *The Negro History Bulletin*, March, 1951, 128–132.

32. *Quarles*, 193, where he points out that in 1788, the New York legislature did permit masters to set free any able-bodied slave under fifty.

33. For an example of a slave used as a trumpeter in an elite militia company see: H. Charles McBarron Jr., Frederick P. Todd, John R. Elting, "Chatham Light Dragoons, Georgia Volunteer Militia, 1811–1816," published in *Military Uniforms in America: Years of Growth, 1796–1851*, edited by John R. Elting from the series produced by the Company of Military Historians, Presidio Press, 1977, 8–9, hereafter *Years of Growth*; Gerard T. Altoff, *Amongst my best men: African-Americans and The War of 1812*, the Perry Group, Put-in-Bay, Ohio, 1996, 67–69.

34. Hugh Hasting, State Historian, *Public Papers of Daniel D. Tompkins, Governor of New York, 1807–1817*, Wynkoop Hallenbeck Crawford Company, State Printers, New York and Albany, 1898, Volume I, 665.

35. *Wilkes*, 66; *Altoff*, 69–70. Unfortunately, to date, not much is known about this "Mr. R. Stevens," other than he might have been a resident of New York City, and was probably a white man.

36. Anthony Gero, "Some Notes on New York's Black Regiments," *Military Collector and Historian*, Journal of the Company of Military Historians, Vol. XXXI, No. 1, Spring 1979, 36. The Martindale quote was in Joseph T. Wilson's *The Black Phalanx*, American Publishing Company, Hartford, 1889, 87–88. Sackett's Harbor was the main American naval base on Lake Ontario.

37. Hugh Hasting, State Historian, *Public Papers of Daniel D. Tompkins, Governor of New York, 1807–1817*, J.B. Lyon Company, State Printer, 1903, Volume III, 585–590, 596, 613–616.

38. For example, John K. Mahon, *The War of 1812*, Gainesville, 1972, is a massive and well-documented history of the entire war; René Chartrand, *Uniforms of the United States Forces in the War of 1812*, Old Fort Niagara, Old Fort Niagara Association Inc., Youngstown, NY, 1992, covers not only the United States Army, but also the state militias during the war.

39. In letters I exchanged in 1975 with Manager Patrick Wilder, Sackett's Harbor Battlefield, he had no evidence on these men. Whether

these black men came to Sackett's Harbor in late 1814, as suggested by Congressman Martingale, is open to debate. See also Patrick A. Wilder, *The Battle of Sackett's Harbour, 1813*, Baltimore, MD: The Nautical and Aviation Publishing Company of America, 1994.

40. Anthony Gero, "A Report of New York Afro-Americans in the War of 1812: August, 1814," *Military Collector and Historian*, Vol. XLIV, No. 3, Fall 1992, 126.

41. For details on Philadelphia's African-Americans building fortifications see *Nell*, 191. Nell says that more than 2,500 African-American citizens came out to work on the defenses; *Wilkes*, 65–66. For an interesting study of African-Americans in New York see: Leo H. Hirsch Jr., "The Negro and New York, 1783–1865," *Journal of Negro History*, Vol. XVI, 1931, 382–473.

42. In Jesse J. Johnson, Lt. Colonel, AUS (Ret.) Editor, *The Black Soldier (Documented) 1619–1815: Missing Pages in United States History*, Hampton Institute, Hampton, Virginia, 1969, on page 69, he quotes a letter written from New York on September 6, 1814. In this letter a "Thos. Lefferts" addressed the U.S. War Department that if black soldiers were raised in New York City he would be willing to serve as a white officer in these units. However, a check of Francis B. Heitman's *Historical Register and Dictionary of the United States Army*, Volume I, Washington DC, Government Printing Office, 1903, and Hugh Hasting (State Historian of NY), *Military Minutes of the Council of Appointments of the State of New York, 1783–1821*, Albany, J.B. Lyon, State Printer, 1902, in five volumes with Index, reveals no Thomas Lefferts being commissioned. Unless new evidence can be found on Mr. Lefferts, it can not yet be said if he commanded any unit.

43. Anthony Gero, "Jordan B. Noble, Black drummer of the Seventh Regiment, U.S. Infantry, 1813 to 1815, "*Military Collector and Historian,* Vol. XXXI, No. 1, Spring 1979, 34, hereafter *Gero: Jordan B. Noble*; Scott S. Sheads, "A Black Soldier Defends Fort McHenry, 1814," *MC&H*, Vol. XLI, No. 1, Spring, 1989, 20.

44. Consult Anthony Gero and Philip G. Maples, "Notes on the Dress of the 13th Regiment, United States Infantry, 1812–1813" *MC&H*, Vol. XLV, No. 4, Winter 1993, 167–168; G. McAlexander, *History of the 13th Regiment United States Infantry*, 1905.

45. Robert Ewell Greene, *Black Defenders of America, 1775–1973*, Johnson Publishing Company Inc., Chicago, 1974, 30–31. Mr. Greene lists many other Regular Army units, whose muster rolls may have had black or mulatto men on them. Research continues on Jacob Dexter.

46. Byron N. Clark (ed.) *A List of Pensioners of the War of 1812: With an Appendix containing names of Volunteers for the defense of Platts-burgh from Vermont towns . . .* Burlington Vermont, 1904, reprinted by the Genealogical Publishing Company, Baltimore, 1969, 129–131. The men are listed as "John Baptist, black; Abraham Derbey, black; Samuel Hatford, black; Nathaniel Lawrence, black; James Millikin, black; Cornelius Melona, black; Samuel W. Marshall, black; Samuel Ridgway, black; Nathaniel Sawyer, black; Robert Thomas, black; Jonathan Townsend, black; Ebenezer Wiman, black; Ezra Wheelock, black." Since these men have first and last names, the probability is that they were freemen. The U.S. Corps of Artificers was a part of the Regular Army, see H. Charles McBarron Jr. and Detmar H. Finke, "U.S. Corps of Artificers, 1812–1815, as published in *Years of Growth*, 44–45. At the time of the publication of McBarron's and Finke's research, I doubt they were familiar with this payroll of Floyd's company. Since these two fine researchers, both known to me, are now deceased, the rediscovery of Floyd's payroll cannot be reviewed by them. In my correspondence with René Chartrand, conducted in 2003–2004, the listing of these black men on Floyd's payroll was brand new data to him. For additional attitudes on these black soldiers, as expressed by General George Izard, see Richard V. Barbuto, *Niagara 1814: America Invades Canada*, University Press of Kansas, 2000, 202–203

47 For several references see *Altoff*, Part I: Chapter 5: The Inland Seas; Anthony Gero, "American Deserter Notices in the Northern Theater, 1813 to 1815" *MC&H*, Vol. XXXVIII, No. 2, Summer 1986, 72–73, in which a "Ten Dollar Reward, Deserted from the United States Flotilla on Lake Champlain, on 28 December 1813, William Fisher, a black man, aged about 27 . . ." is noted.

48. Wilkes, 69–70; *Altoff*, 29; in 1913 at Buffalo, New York, appropriate medals to Anthony Williams service were given his kinsmen Catharine Seaton, Moses Day and C.A. Dickson, see 93–95 of George D. Emerson, *The Perry's Victory Centenary*, Albany, J.B. Lyon Company Printers, 1916.

49. Robin Winks, *The Blacks in Canada: a History*, McGill-Queen University Press, Montreal but published by Yale University Press, New Haven and London, 1971, 150. Winks states that a "Richard Pierpont, (sic)" a black loyalist who had fought in Butler's Rangers, help organize this new black company of 1812. I would assume this is the same man as listed in Cruikshanks' 1893 history. For men of color in the Canadian Voltigeurs consult *Barbuto*, 64–65. For an example of the Royal Marines on the Atlantic coast, see Anthony Gero, "The use of Ex-Slaves in the Royal Marines, circa 1814–1815," *MC&H* Vol. XXXI, No. 4, Winter 1979, 154.

50. *Gero: Jordan B. Noble*; for an official U.S. Army portrait of the Free Men of Color in action at New Orleans, done by the late and prominent American Army illustrator H.C. McBarron Jr., see Brigadier General Harold W. Nelson (USA-Ret.), Editor in Chief, Major General Bruce Jacobs (AUS-Ret), Editor, Colonel Raymond K. Bluhm, Jr. (USA-Ret.), Graphic Editor, *The Army*, The Army Historical Foundation, Beaux Arts Edition, 2001, "Chapter: Patriots All the Time: The Guard and Reserve: Only in America," which has a full-size rendition of this plate originally produced by the Government Printing Office in their series of the U.S. Army military prints; see McConnell for more data on the 7th Regiment and Jordan Noble.

51. For an overall in-depth history of these West India Regiments, consult Roger N. Buckley, *Slaves in Red Coats: The British West India Regiments, 1795–1815*, Yale University Press, 1979.

Chapter 2

1. Carlton Mabee, *Black Education in New York State: From Colonial to Modern Times*, Syracuse University Press, 1979, 17; The New York Manumission Society was established in 1785 with John Jay as its president, Carter G. Woodson, PhD, *The Negro In Our History*, 7th Edition, the Associated Publishers, Inc., Washington, DC, 1941, 131–132; *Berlin and Harris*, "Chapter 4-The Long Death of Slavery," by Patrick Rael, 123–125.

2. Marcus Cunliffe, *Soldiers and Civilians*, Boston, 1968, for valuable information on the militia system and its troubles, 1817–1859 in the United

States; consult also Anthony Gero and Philip G. Maples, "Observations on the Infantry Uniforms of the New York State Militia, 1820–1835," *MC&H*, Vol. XXXVI, No. 4 Winter 1984, 151–151, which has historical data on the role of the NYSM's "common militia;" Anthony Gero and Philip G. Maples, "Fusileering in Western New York, 1830–1840," *MC&H*, Vol. XXXII, No. 3, Fall 1980, 117, which has data on the anti-militia protests in Western NY.

3. Jack D. Foner, *Blacks and the Military in American History: a New Perspective*, Praeger Publishers, New York and Washington, 1974, 26–27.

4. John K. Mahon, *History of the Second Seminole War, 1835–1842*, University of Florida Press, Gainesville, 1967; *Woodson*, 193–198.

5. Thomas S. Lanard, *One Hundred Years with the State Fencibles: a History of the Infantry Corps, Infantry Battalion and Old Guard State Fencibles, 1813–1913*, Nields Company, Philadelphia, 1913, 16–17, 19, 20, 25, 28, 30, 44–45. Johnson's Band was attached to the State Fencibles through most of the 1820s. His band toured in Europe in the 1830s.

6. John R. Elting (Editor), *Military Uniforms in America: Long Endure: The Civil War Period, 1852–1867*, from the series produced by the Company of Military Historians, Presidio Press, 1982, 16 in a uniform study on the 1st Regiment, written and illustrated by H. Charles McBarron Jr., and Frederick P. Todd.

7. *Foner*, 30–31. According to Foner's research, Massachusetts tried in vain to enlist black men into the militia during the 1850s, the last attempt happening in 1858 when the Republican-controlled Massachusetts Legislature passed an act to allow such enlistment, only to have it vetoed by then Governor Nathaniel Banks. For an interesting possibility of a black man serving in the Massachusetts Volunteer Militia consult John O. Curtis, "Jack Lee of Rowley, Massachusetts: A Black New Englander in the Nineteenth Century Massachusetts Militia," *Military Collector and Historian*, Vol. 54, No. 2, Summer 2002, 72–75.

8. In a New York State Senate document, No. 4, from the Adjutant-General's Office, dated January 5, 1832, and in "A Militia Law of the State of New York ... Passed May 13, 1846," and a similar law passed May 13, 1847, it is clear the state was following the 1792 Federal Militia Act; for an 1834 view of the anti-abolitionists demonstrations in New

York City see Colonel Emmons Clark, *History of the Seventh Regiment of New York, 1806–1889*, Volume I, np, 220–222.

9. *Nell*, 130. For a view of Nell's life as an abolitionist and historian, along with a photograph of him, consult Jean Fagan Yellin, *Harriet Jacobs: A Life*, Basic Civitas Books, a member of the Perseus Books Group, 2004.

10. Dudley T. Cornish, *The Sable Arm: Negro Troops in the Union Army, 1861–1865*, W.W. Norton and Company, Incorporated, NY, 1966, 21–22, 253–254.

11. Not having the exact date of the *Tribune* quote is frustrating, see *Foner*, 30.

12. Anthony Gero, "Independent Afro-American Military Companies, 1854–1860: Some Observations," *MC&H*, Vol. XLVI, No. 1, Spring 1992, 8–9.

13. David Ellis; James A. Frost; Harold C. Syrett; Harry F. Carman, *A Short History of New York State*, New York Historical Association, Cornell University Press, Ithaca, NY, Third Printing, 1962, 342; Ernest A. McKay, *The Civil War and New York City*, Syracuse University Press, 1990 has much data on Wood's dubious career, attitudes, and machinations; W.E.B. DuBois, *The Suppression of the African Slave-Trade to the United States of America 1638–1870*, 1896, Schocken Edition, 1969, 143, 178–179; *Berlin and Harris*, "Chapter 9-Southern Slavery In A Free City: Economy, Politics, and Culture," by David Quigley, 275–277.

14. Allan Nevins and Milton Halsey Thomas (Editors), *The Diary of George Templeton Strong: The Civil War, 1860–1866*, the Macmillian Company, New York, 1952, 361; *McKay*, Chapter 11.

15. *Cornish*, 6; James M. McPherson, *The Negroes Civil War: How American Negroes Felt And Acted During The War For The Union*, Vintage Books, a Division of Random House, New York, 1965, 19. The name of the Pittsburgh company was the Hannibal Guards.

16. *Cornish*, 253; *McKay*, 164–168, 178.

17. Colonel Frederick P. Todd's *American Military Equipage, 1851–1872: Volume II: State Forces*, published by Chatham Square Press, Inc, 1983, hereafter *State Forces*. Todd found no records of any sanctioned black militia companies in New York State from 1851 through 1872

18. Brigadier General J. J. Richards, *Rhode Island's Early Defenders and the Successors*, 1937, 62; Luis F. Emilio, *A Brave Black Regiment:*

History of the Fifty-fourth Regiment of Massachusetts Volunteer Infantry, 1863–1865, the Boston Book Company, Boston, 1894, reprinted by Arno Press and the *New York Times*, New York, 1969, 318. Pennsylvania may have had black militia companies from June/July 1863 through 1864, Wilbur Sturtevant Nye, *Here Come The Rebels*, Louisiana State University Press, 1965, reprinted by Morningside House, Inc, 1988, 216–217, 283–284, a copy supplied to me by Roger Sturcke.

19. A Buffalo newspaper called for the recruitment of black soldiers in August of 1862, as cited in *Cornish,* 52. If one cross references this with the men who enlisted in 54th Massachusetts from the Buffalo area, one can assume that enough men could have formed a Buffalo unit in 1860–1862.

20. *Franklin*, 169.

21. *Cornish*, 108–109; Noah Andre Trudeau, *Like Men of War: Black Troops in the Civil War 1862–1865*, Castle Books, Edison, New Jersey, 2002, 7; Berlin and Harris, "Chapter 10—Securing Freedom: The Challenges of Black Life In Civil War New York," by Iver Bernstein, 306–309.

22. *Cornish*, 254. The Superintendent of the Census, Joseph C.G. Kennedy, estimated that New York State's black population in 1860 was 10,208 freemen of color and that about 2,041 would be able to be soldiers; thus the 4,125 men recruited for the 20th and 26th was double his estimate. McKay's research indicates that by 1865, New York City's African-American population had fallen to less than 10,000, 308–309; William Seraile, "The Struggle to Raise Black Regiments in New York State, 1861–1864," the *New York Historical Society Quarterly, Volume LVIII, July 1974, No. 3*, 228. For men who joined outside of designated areas, see *Emilio's* regimental rolls.

23. Anthony Gero and Roger Sturcke, *Cayugans in the Field: 1793–2003, Citizen Soldiers of Cayuga County, New York*, Jacobs Press, Auburn, NY, 2004; in the 1860 and 1865 U.S. Census, provided by Cayuga County Historian Sheila Tucker. William Wise was listed as a freedom seeker from Maryland, residing in Auburn; *Emilio*, 373 for Wise's name in Company G.

24. *Emilio*, 34; for poignant letters from a soldier of the 54th, eventually killed in combat, see Virginia M. Adams (Editor), *On the Altar of Freedom: A Black Soldier's Civil War Letters from the Front-Corporal James Henry Gooding*, the University of Massachusetts Press, 1991; David

P. Krutz, Distant *Drums: Herkimer County, New York in the War of the Rebellion*, North Country Books, 1997, 107; for a vivid account of the 54th Massachusetts at Olustee in 1864, see *Trudeau*, 138–155; the 54th's combat record helped it earn honors into William F. Fox, Lt. Col, U.S.V., *Regimental Losses in the American Civil War, 1861–1865*, Albany Publishing Company, 1893, 423. From all those regiments raised during the war, only 300 regiments made it into Fox's classic work. The two other detailed there are the 8th U.S.C.T. (421) and 79th U.S.C.T. (422).

25. William A. Gladstone, *United States Colored Troops, 1863–1867*, Thomas Publication, 1990. For more on the 54th Regiment's uniforms see Richard Warren, Anthony Gero, Roger Sturcke, "54th Regiment, Massachusetts Volunteer Infantry, 1863–1865," Plate No. 556, as published in *Military Uniforms in America*, by the Company of Military Historians.

26. Joseph T. Glatthaar *Forged in Battle: The Civil War Alliance of Black Soldiers and White Officers*, the Free Press, a Division of Macmillian Inc., 1990; Edwin S. Redkey, *A Grand Army of Black Men, Letters from African-American Soldiers in the Union Army, 1861–1865*, Cambridge University Press, 1992 are excellent studies of the U.S.C.T.

27. *Berlin and Harris*, "Chapter 10-Securing Freedom: The Challenges of Black Life In Civil War New York," by Iver Bernstein, 295–297; *Gladstone* 103: the 31st U.S.C.T. did have large numbers of black New Yorkers in it; Wilson's *Black Phalanx*, 469; Todd's *State Forces*, 1055; C.R. Gibbs, *Black, Copper & Bright (The District of Columbia's Black Civil War Regiment)*, Three Dimensional Publishing, 2002, roster lists 228–259; *Trudeau*, 126, has evidence that Orderly Sergeant Charles Jackson of the 8th U.S.C.T. may have been from New York City.

28. *New York Daily Tribune*, January 13, 1864; the 20th received their colors at Union Square on March 5, 1864, and a woodcut of that was published in *Harper's Weekly*, March 19, 1864; *Seraile*, 230–231. For the 26th's uniforms consult Alan Archambault and Anthony Gero, "United States Colored Troops, Enlisted Men, Infantry, 1864–1865," Plate No. 736 in *Military Uniforms in America*, as published by the Company of Military Historians.

29. Greene's *Black Canadians* has additional information on the role of these volunteers.

30. *The Auburn Daily Advertiser and Union* (Auburn, New York) of March 12 and 21, April 1, 9 and 28, and October 20, 1863, on the recruiting stations set up in Auburn, Oswego, Utica, Rome, Syracuse, Little Falls, Canajoharie, Buffalo, Albany, and New York City. The paper stated agents for the 55th Massachusetts Infantry, 2nd South Carolina Volunteers (34th U.S.C.T.), and 14th Rhode Island Heavy Artillery (Colored) may have recruited in New York State, too.

31. *Emilio*, 339–389; *Trudeau*, 115. 376, 386; *Gladstone*, 26 which has an image of Swails; data on Cornish was supplied by Kaitlyn Greenidge of Historic Weeksville: weeksvillesociety.org

32. *Foner*, 46; *McPherson*, 58–59; Hildegarde Hoyt Swift, *The Railroad to Freedom: A Story of the Civil War*, Hartcourt, Brace and Company, New York, 1932, 293–345, although a fictionalized account, she has an extensive bibliography on Tubman's life; *Woodson*, 234–235.

33. Donald M. Wisnoski, *The Opportunity Is At Hand: Oneida County, New York, Colored Soldiers in the Civil War*, Schroeder Publications, 2003, and Harry Bradshaw Matthews, *Honoring New York's Forgotten Soldiers: African Americans of the Civil War*, Oneonta, New York, 1998.

34. Joan Maynard and Gwen Cottman, *Weeksville, Then and Now*, published by the Society for the Preservation of Weeksville and Bedford-Stuyvesant History, First Printing, 1983; Yellin's *Harriet Jacobs: A Life*.

35. Glenn Coin, "Historians trace unusual photograph to Cazenovia," *The Post Standard,* Syracuse, New York, Monday, July 9, 2007, 1, 4, with an accompanying image from the collection of Angelo Scarlato, that shows Cazenovia GAR Post 160, ca. 1900 with two African-Americans identified by Elyse Luray of Public Broadcasting Service show *History Detective* as being Alberto Robbins and John Stevenson; William R. Cook and Eric C. Huynh, *Around Dansville*, Arcadia Publishing, 2006, 40, shows a black man with the Dansville veterans who could have been a soldier or a subcook of a white New York State regiment; *Gladstone*, 64 on subcooks of African descent on the rolls of other states' white regiments. Whether such happened in New York State is unclear, phone conversations with William Gladstone, winter of 2007, on subcooks; Half-Shire Historical Society, *Northern Oswego County*, Arcadia Publishing, 2003, 114 for an image of Henry F. Roberts, an African-American in the 29th

Connecticut Volunteers, who may have joined the A.J. Barney Post, GAR, Sandy Creek.

36. Prue enlisted at Geneva, New York, but listed Cayuga County as his residence; data supplied by Eileen McHugh, director, Cayuga Museum who found Prue's burial records in the Oakglen Cemetery. The newspaper's photograph caption reads "Civil War Vets-Despite the rapidly diminishing number of Civil war vets, the following eight, range in age from 79 to 8(?), all live in (unreadable) . . . New York. They are, left to right: Thos. Tierney, Edwin U. Hanford, George E. Carr, William Peake, Samuel C. Bradley, Daniel Snuahall, Nathan Prue and Harrison Reed." Prue is the only African-American seen. Another privately held image shows these same veterans, but in a different pose and a copy of that image now resides in the Cayuga Museum's collection.

37. *Cornish*, 253, 255. As a comparison to this New York figure, Cornish lists Massachusetts with 3,966 black soldiers, while Pennsylvania had 8,612 black soldiers accredited to it.

38. *Wilson*, 103; *Foner*, 47–48; Herbert Aptheker, "The Negro in the Union Navy," *Journal of Negro History*, Vol. XXXII, April 1947, 169–200.

39. *McPherson*, 191; *Seraile*, 232–233. Several of the original colors and flags of the 20th and 26th U.S.C.T. are described in Frederick Phisterer's *New York in the War of the Rebellion, 1861–1865*, Albany: L.B. Lyon Company, State Printer,Volume I, 1912, 141.

40. *New York Daily Tribune*, April 26, 1865; it was estimated that more than 200 African-Americans were in the procession, *Berlin and Harris*, "Chapter 10—Securing Freedom: The Challenges of Black Life In Civil War New York," by Iver Bernstein, 323–324.

Chapter 3

1. For the Regular Army's role in Texas see William L. Richter, *The Army in Texas During Reconstruction, 1865–1870*, Texas A&M University Press, College Station, 1987.

2. Jack D Foner, *Blacks and the Military in American History: A New Perspective*, Praeger Publishers, NY and Washington, 1974, 52. Arlen L. Fowler, *The Black Infantry in the West, 1869–1891*, a Negro University

Press Publication, Greenwood Publishing Corporation, Westport, Connecticut, 1972, 12–13; William G. Muller, *The Twenty Fourth Infantry, Past and Present*, reprinted by the Old Army Press, Ft. Collins, Colorado, 1972; William H. Leckie, *The Buffalo Soldiers: A Narrative of the Negro Cavalry in the West*, University of Oklahoma Press, Norman, 1967.

3. *Fowler*, 148; *Foner*, 52–53; see also Muller for early history of the 24th Regiment. One black New Yorker, Sergeant Denny John, 9th U.S. Cavalry, born in Big Flats, New York, was awarded his Medal of Honor on November 27, 1894, *Black Americans in the Defense of Our Nation*, Department of Defense, United States Government Printing Office, 1985, 61, hereafter *Black Americans in the Defense*.

4. *Foner*, 65–66; for an example consult John F. Marszalek, Jr., *Court Martial: The Army Vs. Johnson Whittaker: An Account of the Ordeal of a Black Cadet at West Point in 1881*, Charles Scribner's Sons, 1972. In 1977 a memorial bust to Cadet Flipper was dedicated at the cadet library, see Lt. Colonel (Ret.) Michael Lee Lanning, *The African American Soldier: from Crispus Attucks to Colin Powell*, a Citadel Press Book, 1997, 67. Images of Cadets Flipper, Johnson, and Young appear in *Black Americans in the Defense*, 142–143; Gail Buckley's *American Patriots: The Story of Blacks in the Military from the Revolution to Desert Storm*, Random House, 121–132.

5. *Lanning*, 80–81.

6. *Lanning*, 79–80, a photo of the U.S.S. *Newark*'s crew, circa 1895, shows an integrated crew. Seaman Noil was born in Nova Scotia, but enlisted in New York City, see *Black Americans in the Defense*, 63; *Foner*, 103.

7. Stephen H. Evans, Capt. U.S.C.G, *The United States Coast Guard, 1790–1915, A Definitive History*, United States Naval Institute, Annapolis, Maryland, 1949, 186, which shows the crew of the Practice Cutter *Chase*, about 1906. Several ship stewards, and one sailor, appear to be African-Americans; *Black Americans in the Defense*, 172–175; in 1880, the Pea Island Lifesaving Station, North Carolina, was manned by all black surfmen, *Black Americans in the Defense*, 173–174.

8. Dorothy Sterling (ed.), *The Trouble They Seen: The Story of Reconstruction in the Words of African Americans*, DeCapo Press, New York, 1994, 402–404, 461–469; for a fuller view of this era consult Otis Singletary, *Negro Militia and Reconstruction*, University of Texas Press,

1957; Charles Johnson Jr., *African American Soldiers in the National Guard*, Greenwood Press, Westport, Connecticut, 1992, 20–21, hereafter *African American Soldiers in the National Guard*; Woodson, 415–416, which also has an account of this attack on these black militia men.

9. Martin K. Gordon, "The Black Militia in the District of Columbia," *Records* of the Columbia Historical Society of Washington, DC, 1971–1972, published by the Society, Distributed by the University of Virginia, 1973, 411–420; William B. Gatewood, *Smoked Yankees and the Struggle for Empire: Letters from Negro Soldiers: 1898–1902*, University of Illinois Press, Chicago, 1971, 9; *African American Soldiers in the National Guard*, 21–23; Jim Dan Hill, *The Minute Man in Peace and War: A History of the National Guard*, the Stackpole Company, Harrisburg, Pennsylvania, 1964, 108–119; Thomas G. Rogers, "Georgia's Volunteer Militia, 1872–1898," *Military Collector and Historian*, Volume 59, No. 2, Summer 2007, 89, 98–99.

10. The Capital Guards were designated Company F, see Major Henry H. Nankivell, *History of the Military Organization of the State of Colorado, 1860–1935*, printed 1935, 68; the 2nd Brigade, California Militia, centered around San Francisco, may have had an African-American company, see a lithograph, owned by Mrs. Ann K. Brown, in the *Military Collector and Historian*, March, 1952; *African American Soldiers in the National Guard*, 33.

11. *Gatewood*, 11; *Historical Annual: National Guard and Naval Militia of the State of Ohio*, Army and Navy Publishing Company, Baton Rouge, 1938, which contains the history of the 372nd Infantry's origins that go back to several early Ohio black militia companies; officer's photo, 9th Battalion (Colored), Ohio N.G., circa 1880s, in the Anthony Gero Collection; Alan Archambault and Anthony Gero, "8th Illinois Volunteer Regiment (Infantry), 1898–1899 (Plate No. 620)," *MC&H*, Vol. XL No. 1, Spring 1988; *African American Soldiers in the National Guard*, 24.

12. Major William P. Clarke, *Official History of the Militia and National Guard of the State of Pennsylvania*, Volume III, 1912, 119–171; *Lanard*, 244 on the Gray Invincibles; *American Soldiers in the National Guard*, 27–29.

13. *Richards*, 62, 64, 72–73, 77, 86, by 1887 only the 1st and 2nd Separate Companies, Rhode Island Militia existed; Philip G. Maples and

Anthony Gero, "5th Battalion (Colored), Connecticut National Guard, circa 1879," *MC&H*, Vol. XXXVI, No. 2, Summer 1984, 70–71; Ernest Saunders, *Blacks in the Connecticut National Guard, A pictorial and chronological history, 1870 to 1919*, New Haven Afro-American Historical Society, Inc., New Haven, 1977; *Emilio*, 318; Charles W. Hall (ed.), *Regiments and Armories of Massachusetts*, W.W. Porter Company, Boston, 1899, two volumes, which has data on the Second Battalion (colored) 1862–1876; David C. Abbott and Anthony Gero, "Company L, 6th Massachusetts Volunteer Infantry, 1898–1899 (Plate No. 476)," *MC&H*, Vol. XXX, No. 4, Winter 1978, 184–185; *African American Soldiers in the National Guard,* 30–31.

14. Colonel DeWitt Clinton Falls, *New York Guardsman Magazine* of October, 1928.

15. Although the Griffin Excelsior Guards are undergoing research, Fall's comments on the 15th Regiment still hold true. On April 16, the *New York Times* listed the Griffin Excelsior Guards companies' officers, but did not mention Charles Leslie of the Skidmore Guards among the officers of the Griffin Excelsior Guards. On May 20, 1871, the paper ran an article on page 8, column 2, headlined, "The Colored Voters Exciting Meeting at Morning Star Hall-Tammany Tricks Exposed and Denounced," which may account for why the African-American community of the city, staunch Republicans, rejected the efforts of the Tweed Democrats to establish this black regiment.

16. *Landard*, 244 for the reference on the Veteran Guards as well as in the *New York Times*, July 5, 1876, page 4; additionally, the *New York Times* of July 3, 1876, page 8, states that the "Battalion of Skidmore Guards, Maj. Browne commanding" would be in the July 4 parade in New York City; William J. Simmons, *Men of Mark*, Geo. M. Rewell & Company, 1887, reprinted by Johnson Publishing Co., 659 for the reference on the Shaw Cadets; *Berlin and Harris,* "Chapter 11-Re-Creating Black New York At Century's End," by Marcy S. Sacks, 329.

17. The following paragraphs are reconstructed from my article, Anthony Gero, "The Onondaga Colored Battalion, 1876–1877," *MC&H*, Vol. XXXIV, No. 3, Fall 1982, 117.

18. The source for this reference is a pamphlet entitled "Early Black Syracusans" in the possession of the Onondaga County Historical Association, located in Syracuse, New York. Whether any of the descendants of

this battalion are still living in the Syracuse area is still to be determined. For evidence of previous military service see the roster of Company E, 54th Massachusetts Volunteer Infantry, in *Emilio's* work, 359–363. More than ten members of Company E came from the city of Syracuse.

19. *Gatewood*, 3–18; Lieut. F. E. Edward, *The '98 Campaign of the 6th Massachusetts U.S.V.*, Little, Brown and Company, Boston, 1899. Although Missouri refused to include her African-American citizens in her troop quota for 1898, six hundred men did enlist in the 7th United States Volunteer Infantry, see Lt. Colonel Roger D. Cunningham (USA-Ret.), "Missouri's Black Immunes in the Spanish American War," *Military Collector and Historian*, Washington, DC, Volume 56, No. 1, 2004, 14–23.

20. *Gatewood*, 9; *New York in the Spanish American War 1898, in Three Volumes,* James B. Lyon, State Printer, Albany, 1900; Benjamin R. Beede (Editor), *The War of 1898 and U. S. Interventions 1898–1934: An Encyclopedia*, Garland Publishing, Inc., 1994.

21. The regiment left the Philippines in early 1908 and was posted in upstate New York until 1912, when it was rotated back to the P.I., *Muller*, sections on 1908–1912, which have no page numbers. Muller's work has no rosters either so researching New Yorkers in the 24th depends on genealogical data from other sources. There is evidence that black New Yorkers served as company stewards and servants in some New York units, consult Colonel Frederick P. Todd and Major Kenneth C. Miller, *Pro Patria et Gloria: The illustrated story of one hundred and fifty years of the Seventh Regiment of New York*, Rampart House, Hartsdale, NY, 1956, in the section entitled "Customs and Traditions;" Nancy L. Todd, *New York's Historic Armories: An Illustrated History*, State University of New York, 2006, 86.

22. Margaret Hindle Hazen and Robert M. Hazen, *The Music Men: An Illustrated History of Brass Bands in America, 1800–1920*, Smithsonian Institution, 1987, 194; in a 2001 visit to Cornell, I was given a tour of Barton Hall to conduct research on the Cornell Cadet Corps. The names of bandsmen were not listed on the original band photograph and records have yet to be found on who they were. For a short history of the Cornell's cadet corps see, Anthony Gero, "The Cornell Cadet Corps, 1869–1929," *MC&H*, Vol. 53, No. 1, Spring 2001, 33–35; in 1906, African-American students at Cornell organized their own fraternity, Alpha Phi Alpha, see

Rayford W. Logan, *The Betrayal of the Negro from Rutherford B. Hayes to Woodrow Wilson*, New Enlarged Edition, Collier Books, 1965, 343–344.

23. *A Short History*, 454.

24. For an example of this migrations' impact in Chicago see, Horace R. Cayton and St. Clair Drake, *Black Metropolis*, Jonathan Cape, London, 1946. During the period of 1914–1918, with European migration stopped by World War 1, the migration of African-Americans to America's urban centers, like Chicago, was felt even more, see Chapter 3 of Cayton's and St. Clair's book for the impact in that city.

25. *Hirsch*, 382–473.

26. Steven Jantzen, *Hooray for Peace, Hurrah for War, the United States During World War 1*, Times Mirror, NY and Scarborough, Ontario, 1971, 224–225, 228–229.

27. Philip T. Drothing, *Black Heroes in Our Nation's History*, Washington Square Press, New York, second printing, 1971, 152.

28. *Logan*, 362–364; David M. Kennedy, *Over Here: The First World War and American Society*, Oxford University Press, 1980, 281.

29. *Franklin*, 454; *Logan*, 363–370; W.M. Trotter headed the protests by the NAACP and the Equal Rights League, but was rebuffed by President Wilson, *Woodson*, 489–490.

30. *Franklin*, 454.

31. Eventually Bullard joined the French aviator corps and flew combat missions in a plane "marked with a heart pierced by an arrow with the motto: 'All Blood Runs Red,'" *Black Americans in the Defense*, 31; a photograph of Bullard appears in Buckley's *American Patriots*.

32. In an article entitled "New Negro Troops Parade In Fifth Av.," the *New York Times* of October 2, 1916, page 22, column 4, describes the presentation of the colors to the 15th Regiment. The ceremony was held in front of the historic Union Club. Chronologically, the "birth" of the regiment began by a New York State Legislative act, Chapter 793, Laws of 1913, which called for the formation of "A colored regiment of infantry in the City of New York." The formal acceptance of the 15th Regiment was not achieved until 1916 with the presentation of the 15th regiment's colors. It would appear that the Adjutant General dragged his feet on the regiment's formation and used the excuse of not being able to find enough qualified African-Americans as officer candidates who could pass

an officer's Examining Board, consult the *Annual Report of the Adjutant of the State of New York, For the Year 1914*, J.B. Lyon Printers, Albany, 1915, 4, a copy supplied to me by Roger Sturcke.

Chapter 4

1. *Franklin*, 454.

2. *Kennedy*, 29–30.

3. William Loren Katz, *Eyewitness: The Negro in American History*, Pitman Publishing Corporation, NY, 1969, 393.

4. *Kennedy*, 160.

5. *Franklin*, 457.

6. *Drothing*, 153; *Barbeau and Henri*, pp. 70 and 220. The actual figure on blacks in the National Guard is open to some debate, but Barbeau and Henri state that Scott gave the figure at 10,000 in 1917; Roger D. Cunningham, "The Virginia Militia at the National Drill, 1887," *Virginia Cavalcade, Volume 49, Autumn, 2000, Number 4*, 187.

7. *Franklin*, 458; *Foner*, 124; for a sample of the role of African-American women in World War I see: Addie W. Hunton and Kathryn M. Johnson, *Two Colored Women With the American Expeditionary Forces*, Brooklyn Eagle Press, Brooklyn, New York 1920; hereafter *Hunton and Johnson;* W. Allison Sweeney, *History of the American Negro in the Great World War*, Chicago, 1919, 251–252. Sweeney also has many photographs of African-American women during the war.

8. *Kennedy*, 162.

9. *Kennedy*, 161. Only a single group of 639 officers graduated from this facility. Black officers of major and colonel rank were rare in World War I. For a listing of officers graduated from Des Moines see Sweeney, 119–130, for example, Joseph E. Trigg, a captain, and Everett B. Williams, a First Lieutenant, both from Syracuse, New York, were commissioned. For data on early Syracusans see Barbara Sheklin Davis, *Syracuse African Americans*, Arcadia Publishing, 2005.

10. Donald Smythe, *Guerrilla Warrior, the Early Life of John J. Pershing*, New York, 1973.

11. John J. Pershing, *My Experience in the World War*, Volume 1 and 2, Frederick A. Stokes Company, New York, 1931, Volume 2, 116–117, hereafter *Pershing, Volume . . .*

12. *Pershing Volume 1*, 268–269.

13. *Barbeau and Henri*, 18–19; for the record of Edward Harrison Tucker see *Columbia in the World War* by the Home Defense Committee of Columbia County, New York, J.B. Lyon, Albany, NY, 1924, 806; *Pershing, Volume 2*, 118–119.

14. *Barbeau and Henri*, 18.

15. *Pershing, Volume 1*, 291.

16. *Franklin*, 475.

17. Emmett Scott, Special Assistant to the Secretary of War, *Scott's Official History of the American Negro in the World War*, 1919, 346.

18. *Scott,* 346; 375–376; see also Gary Mead, *The Doughboys: America and the First World War*, the Overlook Press, Woodstock, NY, 2000 for additional data on Creel, the CPI and race relations see 375–376.

19. *Scott*, 353.

20. Florette Henri, *Bitter Victory, A History of Black Soldiers in World War I*, Zenith Books, Garden City, NY, 1979, 85.

21. *Scott*, 353; the leaflet's full quote can be found in *Hunton and Johnson*, 53–54.

22. *Scott*, 354; *Franklin*, p. 475; *Pershing Volume 2*, 116–117; Ulysses Lee, *United States Army in World War 2: Special Studies: The Employment of Negro Troops*, Office of the Chief of Military History, U.S. Army, Washington, DC, 1966, 12.

23. Arthur W. Little, *From Harlem to the Rhine: The Story of New York's Colored Volunteers*, Corvice and Friede Publishing, NY, 1936, front listing; *Scott*, 197; *Barbeau and Henri*, 71; Laurence Stallings, *The Doughboys: the Story of the AEF, 1917–1918*, Harper and Row, 1963, 311. For a uniform study of the 369th see Raymond Johnson's "369th U.S. Infantry, New York National Guard, 1918," in *Military Uniforms in America, Volume IV: The Modern Era from 1868*, John R. Elting and Mike McAfee, Editors, Presidio Press, 1988, 96–97; *African American Soldiers in the National Guard*, 79–83.

24. *Little*, ix–x.

25. *Little*, 13–14; *Barbeau and Henri*, 71; *Stallings*, 311. Captain Fish was one of Harvard's great football players and was known throughout the county as such. For data on Lt. Holden's service with the 369th see Christopher L. Kolakowski, "A Sister's Journey to the Western Front in 1920," *MC&H*, Vol. 56, No. 3, Fall 2004, 163, footnote #18.

26. *Little*, 372; *Stallings*, 312; *Hunton and Johnson*, 69; *Sweeney*, photographs between 224–225.

27. *Stallings*, 311–314.

28. *Barbeau and Henri*, 71; *Little*, 7.

29. *Barbeau and Henri*, 71; *Stallings*, 311.

30. *Barbeau and Henri*, 71; *Little*, 42–44, 46.

31. *Barbeau and Henri*, 72; *Little*, 46–47; *Sweeney* has several interesting photographs of this homecoming parade which shows the regiment and band on Lenox Avenue in New York City.

32. *Little*, 46–47.

33. *Little*, 57.

34. *Little*, 71; *Henri*, 43–44.

35. *Barbeau and Henri*, 70, 111–112; *Kennedy*, 175–176. For some history of the 371st Infantry Regiment's service with the French see: Barry Thompson, Orton Begner, Anthony Gero, "371st Infantry Regiment, 93rd Division, 1917–1919, Plate No. 488," *MC&H*, Volume XXXI, No. 3, Fall 1979, 130–131. Note the 371st was a drafted regiment, not made up of guardsmen.

36. *Pershing, Volume 1*, 291.

37. *Foner*, 121; *Barbeau and Henri*, 111.

38. *Foner*, 121–122.

39. *Little*, 109–110; *Stallings*, 312; for a brief summary of Europe's short life, see Howard Dodson, Christopher Moore, Roberts Yancy, *The Black New Yorkers: The Schomburg Illustrated Chronology*, John Wiley & Sons, Inc, 2000, 431, hereafter *Schomburg Illustrated*. Europe had moved to New York State in 1903, help organize the famous Clef Club in 1910, and in 1912, organized a black orchestra which played at Carnegie Hall; *Buckley*, 191–195.

40. *Little*, 184–186; *Stallings*, 322.

41. *Barbeau and Henri*, 116.

42. *Barbeau and Henri*, 117; *Little*, 194–199; *Stallings*, 320–321; Wilhemina S. Robinson, *Historical Negro Biographies*, under the auspices of the Association for the Study of Negro Life and History, Publisher Company, Incorporated, 1967, 212; for a photograph of Roberts see, Kai Wright, *Soldiers of Freedom: An Illustrated History of African Americans in the Armed Forces*, Black Dog & Leventhal, 2002, 142; *Buckley*, 220; *Sweeney*,

146–148, Sweeney states "Johnson was the first private of any race in the American army to get the palm with his Croix de Guerre."

43. *Stallings*, 321.

44. *Barbeau and Henri*, 117. Cobb also wrote of the men of the 369th and 371st Infantry that "They were soldiers who wore their uniforms with a smartened pride; who were jaunty and alert and prompt in their movements. . . . (and they just wanted to) get a whack at the foe with the shortest possible delay," quoted in *Sweeney*, 148.

45. *Lee*, 6–7.

46. *Lee*, 6–7.

47. *Barbeau and Henri*, 116.

48. *Barbeau and Henri*, 118–119. Research continues to see if this Captain Charles Fillmore is the same man who tried to organize a black unit in New York State in 1913.

49. *Sweeney*, 151–152; *Scott*, 210–211.

50. *Sweeney*, 149.

51. *Barbeau and Henri*, 105 and 167; *Little*, 103.

52. *Scott*, 213.

53. *Scott*, 279–280.

54. *Katz*, 394; *Drothing*, 156; *Franklin*, 462–463; *Hill*, 276–278. For some details on a black baseball player, Spottswood Poles, who served in the 369th and won five battle stars and the Purple Heart see Neil Lanctot, *Fair Dealings and Clean Playing: The Hillsdale Club and the Development of Black Professional Baseball, 1910–1932*, McFarland and Company, Inc., Jefferson, North Carolina, 1994, 247, footnote 3 where Lanctot quotes data from Harold Seymour's *Baseball: The People's Game*, New York Oxford University Press, 1990. Despite the gallantry of black soldiers in the AEF, no Congressional Medal of Honors were awarded to any African-American during the war, nor were any awarded during World War II. For a list of officers and men of the 369th who were presented Croix de Guerre in World War I consult *Sweeney*, 142–145.

55. *Lee*, 7.

56. *Little*, 191; *Schomburg Illustrated*, 162. Recently, *Military Images* magazine published a complete issue, "African-Americans In The Great War: 1917–1919," Volume XXVII, Number 4, Jan/Feb., 2006. On pages 12–13 were images from the Bruce Jarvis Collection of bandsmen of the

369th while in France which, I believe, were previously unpublished or rarely seen.

57. *Kennedy*, 162.

58. *Scott*, 190–191.

59. *Scott*, 191–192, 195.

60. *Scott*, 191–192.

61. *Scott*, 192; *Barabeau and Henri*, 84; *Kennedy*, 239–240.

62. *Barbeau and Henri*, 65.

63. *Barbeau and Henri*, 142.

64. *Katz*, 393–394. The original letter was written by Howard H. Long and was published in his article "The Negro Soldier in the Army of the United States," *Journal of Negro Education*, Vol. 12, Summer, 1943, 311–312.

65. *Scott*, 175; *Henri*, 97, 101.

66. *Sweeney*, 212.

67. *Scott*, 183.

68. *Barbeau and Henri*, 170–171.

69. Maurice DeCastelbled, *History of the AEF, compiled from records of the War Department Order of Battle of the United States Land Forces in the World War, and from the Final Report of General John J. Pershing*, Bookcraft, New York, 1937, 155; *Barbeau and Henri*, 171. As an example of how the reputation of the 92nd Division was belittled even as the war was being fought, see *Franklin*, 469.

70. Other regions in the state need to be researched. For instance in a booklet entitled, *Madison County's Welcome Home*, published by *The Oneida Dispatch Press*, Oneida, New York, 1919, an original copy in my collection, has a photo of Madison County's Third Contingent of drafted men (Nov. 23, 1917) on page 35. In the group are two men who appear to be African-Americans. On page 78, is a photo of an officer, First Lieutenant John Powless of Oneida, who may also be African-American.

71. *Cayugans in the Field*, 23; see Gerald W. Patton, *War and Race: The Black Officer in the American Military, 1915–1941*, Greenwood Press, 1981, 70, hereafter *War and Race*. Patton lists those units at Camp Upton as: the 184th Infantry Brigade Headquarters, 351st Machine Gun Battalion (3 Companies), attached Sanitary Troops and the 367th Infantry Regiment, with attached Sanitary Troops. In total 100 officers and 4,300 men of

African-American descent. The probability of black Cayugans who were assigned to Camp Upton in the 92nd Division is quite high then.

72. *Cayugans in the Field*, 22.

73. *The Citizen-Advertiser*, Auburn, New York, Saturday, June 8, 1935, 5 and April 24, 1945, 10, each had articles on Elmer Carter who eventually rose to prominence in the Urban League and New York State Council. Data on these newspaper articles was provided by Mrs. Mary Gilmore, Seymour Library's History Room, Seymour Library, Auburn, New York, in 2004; see also *Cayugans in the Field*, 24.

74. *Cayugans in the Field*, 23.

75. *Cayugans in the Field*, 23; a new study of the Underground Railroad in Cayuga County undertaken by Professor Judith Wellman and Cayuga County Historian Sheila Tucker has seen several new sites nominated for inclusion on the Underground Railroad, such as Auburn State Prison, the Seward Mansion, plus several local churches. For the information on these sites and those freedom seekers who settled in Cayuga County and served in the Civil War consult Judith Wellman, Project Coordinator, *Uncovering the Freedom Trail in Auburn and Cayuga County, New York: A Cultural Resource Survey*, sponsored by the City of Auburn Historic Resources Review Board and the Cayuga County Historian's Office, Historical New York Research Associates, Fulton, New York, 2005.

76. *Kennedy*, 288; *Mead*, "Chapter 18: The Cost" where he explores the ramifications of World War I for the United States. In this chapter he documents the number of American deaths due to the war as compared to the other Allied Powers, to dollars expended, and the loss of civil liberties at home.

77. *War and Race*, 134, 149.

Chapter 5

1. *Sweeney*, 271.

2. *Katz*, 410–411. For a contemporary account of this parade see *Sweeney*, 267–274 who quotes *The World,* of New York City for February 18, 1919. Sweeney notes that at the rear of the 369th's column were more than 200 wounded soldiers, chauffeured in automobiles, and which showed, in visible features, the cost of modern warfare.

3. *Lee*, 8.

4. *Sweeney*, 152. Sweeney also lists by name on 142–145 all the officers and men of the 369th who were awarded the Croix de Guerre for gallantry in action.

5. *Franklin*, 478.

6. *Barbeau and Henri*, 178; *Kennedy*, 285–286; *Foner*, 126–127; *Henri*, 113–115 and 118; for a vivid description of the Washington, DC attacks consult *Woodson*, 527–529. According to some sources, 2,500 reported cases of lynchings took place in the nation from 1885 to 1900, *Yellin*, 256, which, obviously, set a tone for the Red Summer of 1919.

7. *Scott*, 467–468.

8. *Barbeau and Henri*, 174 and 188; *Henri*, 114; *War and Race*, 148, 155. Patton notes that in Philadelphia, the G.T. Cornish Post #292, of the Lincoln Legion was very active against the exclusion of African-Americans from the CMTC.

9. *Barbeau and Henri*, 114–115.

10. *Barbeau and Henri*, 167; *War and Race*, 110–111.

11. *Franklin*, 469. Moton found that in the division's 12,000 men, only seven had been reported for rape and of the two found guilty, General Headquarters had turned down their convictions; *War and Race*, 103–110.

12. Irvin H. Lee, *Negro Medal of Honor Men*, Dood, Meade and Company, NY, 1967, 105–106.

13. *Lee*, 18.

14. *Lee*, 9–10, 12–14; *Mead*, 415 where he comments on the Army's 1925 Report called "Employment of Negro Man Power in War."

15. Major General Robert Lee Bullard, U.S.A. (Ret.), *Personalities and Reminiscences of the War*, Doubleday, Page and Company, 1925, 296–297; *War and Race*, 146–147; *Mead*, 345–346.

16. *Lee*, 15.

17. *Foner*, 126–127; *Kennedy*, 367–369.

18. *War and Race*, 147, 155. Congressman Fish had been awarded a Silver Star for his service in France with the 369th; Patricia W. Romero, Editor, *International Library of Afro-American Life and History, I Too Am American: Documents from 1619 to the Present*, Volume I, The Association for the Study of Afro-American Life and History, 1978, 214–215.

19. According to a Goggle search at the New York City Depart-ment of Parks and Recreation's Web site, the Edgecombe Avenue Block Association helps maintain Dorrance Brooks Square. According to the Web site posting, more than 10,000 people attended the 1925 ceremony, which included Mayor John F. Hylan and Colonel William Hayward.

20. James A. Sawicki, *Infantry Regiments of the US Army*, Wyvern Publications, 1981, 525–526; *Todd's* New York's Historic Armories, 266–268.

21. *Kennedy*, 244.

22. For a brief history of the 369th, see Colonel DeWitt Clinton Falls, *New York Guardsman Magazine* of October, 1928. Additional information on the 369th in the 1920s is in Michael D. Doubler and John W. Listman Jr., *The National Guard: An Illustrated History of America's Citizen-Soldiers*, Brassey's Inc., Washington, DC, 2003, 69, which shows a photograph of Sgt. Gillard Thompson, bandmaster of the 369th Infantry Band, circa 1924; *African American Soldiers in the National Guard*, 126–131.

23. *War and Race*, 137, 160.

24. *Lanning*, 211–213; Henry I. Shaw Jr. and Ralph W. Donnelly, *Blacks in the Marine Corps*, History and Museums Division, Headquarters, U.S.M.C., Washington, DC, 1975, which covers their history from 1942 through 1975.

25. For an example of an segregated unit in Iowa in the 1930s, see Robert V. Morris, *Tradition and Valor: a Family Journey*, Sunflower University Press, Manhattan, Kansas, 1999. Morris is the Executive Director of the Fort Des Moines Black Officers Memorial, Inc. His grandfather, James Brad Morris Sr., graduated as an officer from the Des Moines school and served in the 92d Infantry Division in World War I.

26. *War and Race*, 140–141, 143, 153.

27. For observations about the CCC see *Katz*, 442–443; *Foner*, 128–129; *Lee*, 54. For comments on Marcus Garvey's movement see *Schomburg*, 150–151 and *Franklin*, 489–493. For the contributions of the Provisional Committee for the Defense of Ethiopia, the Ethiopian World Federation, and the Black Legion, *Schomburg*, 236. African-Americans also volunteered during the Spanish Civil War, see *Wright*, 149–151; for the stories of Vaughn Love and Oliver Law, who served in the Abraham Lincoln Brigade, and of nurse Salaria Kee, consult *Buckley*, 239–255.

28. *Schomburg*, 234. Council members were Robert C. Weaver, Mary McLeod Bethune, Lawrence Augustus Oxley, William Johnson Trent Jr., Eugene Kinckle Jones, and Frank S. Horne.

29. *Foner*, 129–132.

30. Marvin E. Fletcher, *America's First Black General, Benjamin O. Davis, Sr., 1880–1970*, University Press of Kansas, 1989, 80–81. In June 1936 Colonel Davis's son, Benjamin O. Davis Jr., was the first black cadet to graduate from West Point since 1889, *Foner*, 130; *Schomburg*, 240.

31. *Fletcher*, 80–83.

32. *Lee*, 327.

Chapter 6

1. *Franklin*, 574–575.

2. Many books have been written on World War II, but one that can represent what this generation accomplished is Tom Brokaw, *The Greatest Generation*, Random House, New York, 1998. The stories of Martha Settle Putney (Women's Army Auxiliary Corps) and Johnnie Holmes (761st Tank Battalion), African-American veterans, especially relate to *Black Soldiers of New York State*.

3. *Lee*, 24–30, for a comprehensive study on African-American involvement in the Regular Army, the ROTC, the National Guard, the CMTC, and high school cadets.

4. *Lee*, 37–50, for the United States Army's Plans of 1937 and 1940 for the use of black soldiers; see also *Foner*, chapter 7; *Lanning*, chapters 10, 11, and 12; Marvin A. Kreidberg, Lt-Colonel and Merton G. Henry, First Lieutenant, *History of Military Mobilization in the United States Army, 1775–1945*, Department of the Army, November 1955, 643–644.

5. *Franklin*, 580–591; *Foner*, chapter 7; *Lanning*, chapters 10, 11, 12; *Wright*, chapter 6. For a recent history of African-Americans in the 51st and 52nd Defense Battalions, U.S.M.C. consult George Forty, *US Marine Corps Handbook, 1941–1945*, Sutton Publishing Limited, United Kingdom, 2006, 26, 77, 84–85, 93, 96.

6. *Schomburg*, 250; *Katz*, 449. Tragically in 1950, Dr. Drew died in North Carolina while being taken to a black hospital since he had

been turned away from a white hospital. Cause of death was reported due to a loss of blood.

7. *Lee*, 66; Congressman Fish was a staunch support for more involvement of black Americans in the military in the 1930s, *War and Race*, 147, 164–165 for examples of his activities.

8. *Lee*, 78–82. It is interesting to note that according to Foner, of the 776 U.S. generals in World War II, General Davis was the only African-American general during the war; *Foner*, 150–151. During 1870 to 1874, ten black generals had been appointed in the South Carolina militia, but Davis was the first Regular Army general, *Blacks in the Defense*, 111.

9. *Lee*, his Index on the 92nd and 93rd Divisions' history; Lou Potter with William Miles and Nina Rosenblum, *Liberators: Fighting on Two Fronts In World War II*, Harcourt Brace Jovanovich, NY, 1992, 84 for pictures of McConnell and Smith; for a different McConnell image see *Buckley* under illustrations; Charles E. Francis, First Lieut. U.S. Air Force (Reserve), *The Tuskegee Airmen: The Story of the Negro in the U.S. Air Force*, Brice Humphries, Inc., Publishers, Boston, 1955, 204–213 for New York officers and enlisted men killed. One example was "Lieut. Leland H. Pennington, Rochester, New York. Failed to return from mission to Yugoslavia. Suffered with appendicitis may have been cause of death;" Gwendolyn Midlo Hall (ed.), *Love, War, the 96th Engineers (Colored)*, University of Illinois Press, 1995. Some other examples are the hard-luck 2nd Cavalry Division, Horse (Colored) broken up in 1944, the 555th Infantry (Airborne) Battalion, and the 969th Field Artillery Battalion, which help defend Bastogne.

10. For a brief history of the 369th between 1920 and 1940 see Paul H. Till, "NYNG and NYG Insignia, Part V," *Trading Post (ASMIC TP), October–December 1985*, 57–58, a copy supplied by Company of Military Historian's Fellow Roger Sturcke. According to Till's research, the 369th Infantry (Colored) was changed to 269th CA, AA (Colored) upon federalization in 1940; see also data supplied on the 369th Infantry by Company of Military Historian's Fellow Rick Ugino from the New York State Military Museum and Veterans Research Center: http://www.dmna.state.ny.us/historic/reghist/wwi/infantry/369th Inf/369thInfMain.htm.

11. George A. Reed and Carole Reed, *Images of America: Fort Ontario: Guardian of the North*, Arcadia Publishing, Charleston, SC, 2000, 77 and 78; *African African American Soldiers in the National Guard*, 146–147; James J. Cummings, "The Black 369th in Oswego(1941)," *Journal 1972*, Oswego County Historical Society, Oswego, New York, 1973, 55–69; *Oswego Palladium Times*, May 17 and March 11, 1941 found at "Old Fulton NY Post Cards" Web site.

12. *Lee*, 198, 201, 370; Shelby L. Stanton, Captain, USA (Ret.), *World War II: Order of Battle*, Galahad Books, NY, 1984, 452, 472, 496, 602.

13. Karl D. Hartzell, PhD, *The Empire State at War: World War II, Compiled and Written for the New York State War Council*, published by the State of New York, 1949, 91–92; for examples on units of the New York Guard consult: Raymond Johnson and Rick Ugino, "21 Regiment, New York Guard, 1940–1945," MUIA plate #548, *MC&H, Vol. XXXV, No. 4, Winter, 1983; Cayugans in the Field*, for details on Company I, 3rd Regiment, NYG, 29.

14. For example, in the Maryland State Defense Force, the 11th Infantry Battalion (Baltimore) was African-American: see CPT Merle T. Cole, MDSG "Maryland's State Defense Force," *MC&H Vol. XXXIX No. 4, Winter 1987*, 152–157.

15. I had not been aware of Till's fine work on the 15th Regiment, NYG's distinctive insignia and history when I first found the *New York Times* articles. From Till's work, and material supplied by Rick Ugino, it appears that an African-American NYG unit may also have been formed in the 1917–1919 period, see *Sawicki*, 525 where he states, that on July 31, 1918, a 15th Regiment of the New York Guard was formed from depot elements of the 15th Infantry, NY, NG, which had been federalized. Research on the entire NYG in the years 1917 to 1919 continues.

16. Upstate cities and areas that had substantial African-American populations, such as Syracuse, Rochester, and Buffalo, did not have segregated NYG units. This newspaper article indicates why, that is the segregationist policies of the NYG, which confined units to the New York City area.

17. For a brief example on the Harlem "riot," which claimed six lives and saw 185 people injured; see *Schomburg*, 258. The year 1943 was another period for racial violence, with major disturbances taking place in Detroit, Mobile, and Beaumont, Texas.

18. I interpret that sentence to mean all NYG regiments, so one can assume that from August 1944, a machine gun platoon was maintained in the 15th Regiment as well. On August 6, 1944, 32, column 3, the *New York Times* reported, in an article entitled "Training for Guard Praised," that "A group of officers and men receive an intensive course of instruction with the weapon to enable them to carry out instructions in their armoires during the Winter months . . ."

19. This *New York Times* article said that these units arrived "fully equipped with .30 caliber rifles, machine guns and grenades . . ." It also lists all regimental and battalion staff officers for the 15th and 3rd Separate Battalion, but not for the First Platoon, Company B, an unfortunate omission for future researchers. For a full list of the names and ranks of all the officers of the 15th Regiment and 3rd Separate Battalion consult the aforementioned September 1946 article.

20. A Quartermaster company was formed in the NYG in 1945 and on May 18, 1945, the *New York Times* reported, on page 16, column 5, that: "Quartermaster Unit in Guard: The Federal Government has supplied the New York Guard with equipment for a new unit, the First Quartermaster Depot Company, it was announced yesterday. The company, to be composed of nine officers and 108 enlisted men, will include warehouse men, butchers, requisition clerks, food inspectors, chauffeurs and mechanics. They will use the armory at Thirty-fourth Street and Park Avenue."

21. The Regular Army had experimented with segregated platoons in rifle companies in some Infantry Divisions in the European Theater of Operations during 1945. For some examples see: MUIA plate No. 607, by Raymond Johnson and Anthony Gero, "78th Division, Field Uniforms, 1943–1945," *MC&H, Vol. XXXIX, No. 2, Summer 1987* and Anthony Gero and Raymond Johnson, "A Brief Sketch of the Afro-American Combat Volunteers, 104th Infantry Division, 1945," *MC&H*, Vol. XXXIX, No. 2, Summer 1987; *Lee*, Chapter XXII: Volunteer Infantry Replacements; *Lanning*, 181–182; for a view of Wright's military service consult *Buckley*, 324–327. After his eventual return to New York State, Wright went to college on the GI Bill, finished his degree, and finally became a New York State Supreme Court judge.

22. For an account on the disbanding of the NYG refer to the July 8, 1949, issue of the *New York Times*, page 12, column 5. The paper does have several other small articles on these two African-American

units in 1947 and 1948, but they did not shed much knowledge on these two units' history. Note, eventually, the NYG was reconstituted during the 1950s and still continues today as part of the military forces of the Empire State.

23. *Cayugans in the Field*, 27–30.

24. On March 5, 1942, the *Citizen-Advertiser* printed this small item: "Honor Willard Hardy Tonight—A supper and program will be sponsored this evening at the Booker T. Washington Community Center by the Harriet Tubman Young People's Society in Honor of Willard Hardy of 72 Chapman Avenue, who is soon to report for service . . . Hardy was at one time president of the Young People's Society. A large number of the young man's friends have been invited. Lawrence B. Lathrop of 231 East Genesee Street, president of Henderson and Lathrop, automobile dealers, by whom Hardy was formerly employed, will speak."

25. Scott Rapp, "Slain Soldier Honored: Man was Cayuga County's only black soldier killed in World War II," *The Post-Standard, Cayuga Neighbors Section*, Thursday, November 18, 2004, 3–4.

26. *Schomburg*, 262–263; Arnold Rampersad's *Jackie Robinson: a biography*, Alfred A. Knopf, New York, 1997, chapters 5, 6, and 7.

27. *Franklin*, Chapter XXX; *Lanning*, Chapter 13 and Chapter 14; *Foner*, Chapter 8.

28. *Schomburg*, 275; *Lanning*, 228; *Wright*, Chapter 7; the quote on Private Thompson is in *Black America in Defense*, 66; a photograph of Thompson appears in *Buckley's* history; *Negro Medal of Honor Men*, 9–12.

29. In World War I, a good case for the Medal of Honor could be made for Henry Johnson's actions with the 369th Infantry but, at the time, no Medal of Honor was awarded to any black serviceman. In 1997 several African-American soldiers were presented the Medal of Honor for their service in World War II. Among those was Sergeant Edward A. Carter Jr., whose bravery with the 56th Armored Infantry Battalion, 12th Armored Division in March 1945 was finally acknowledged, see Allene G. Carter and Robert L. Allen, *Honoring Sergeant Carter: Redeeming a Black World War II Hero's Legacy*, Amistad, an Imprint of Harper Collins, Publishers, 2003. Regrettably, Sergeant Carter was not alive at the time of

the ceremony so his medal was presented to his family. For images of the Medal of Honor recipients at this ceremony see *Buckley,* photographs.

Chapter 7

1. *Fletcher*, 153, where he notes that in 1947, General Davis, unsuccessfully, encouraged General William Kelly, chief of staff of New York's National Guard to bring about its integration.

2. *War and Race*, 168.

3. *Franklin*, 608; *War and Race*, 137 and 151 on the role of the NAACP in decrying the segregation in the United States military as early as 1921. For a more personal view of how World War II and American-style racism affected his family and helped contribute to the death of his brother, Buck Franklin Jr., an Army veteran, in 1947, see John Hope Franklin's *Mirror to America: The Autobiography of John Hope Franklin*, Farrar, Straus and Giroux, 2005, 4, 86, 101, 103, 105–109, 110, 118–119, 128, 130, 206.

4. *War and Race*, 132, quoting W. E. B. Dubois, "Returning Soldiers," *Crisis 18* (May 1919).

5. Robert Andrews, *The Concise Columbia Dictionary of Quotations*, Avon Book, 1987, 122.

6. Ibid., 167.

Bibliography

Books/Booklets

Adams, Virginia M. (ed.). *A Black Soldier's Civil War Letters from the Front-Corporal James Henry Gooding*. Amherst: University of Massachusetts Press, 1991.

Altoff, Gerard T. *Amongst my best men: African-Americans and the War of 1812*. Put-in-Bay, Ohio: The Perry Group, 1996.

Annual Report of the Adjutant of the State of New York, For the Year 1914. Albany: J.B. Lyon Printers, 1915.

Barbeau, Arthur and Florette Henri. *The Unknown Soldier: Black American Troops in World War I*. Philadelphia: Temple University Press, 1974.

Barbuto, Richard V. *Niagara 1814: America Invades Canada*. University Press of Kansas, 2000.

Beede, Benjamin R. (ed.). *The War of 1898 and U.S. Interventions 1898–1934: An Encyclopedia*. New York: Garland Publishing, Inc., 1994.

Berlin, Ira and Leslie M. Harris (eds.). *Slavery in New York*. USA: The New Press in conjunction with the New York-Historical Society, 2005.

Black Americans in the Defense of Our Nation. Washington, DC: Department of Defense, United States Government Printing Office, 1985.

Brokaw, Tom. *The Greatest Generation*. New York: Random House, 1998.

Buckley, Gail. *American Patriots: The Story of Blacks in the Military from the Revolution to Desert Storm*. New York: Random House, 2001.

Buckley, Roger N. *Slaves in Red Coats: The British West India Regiments, 1795–1815*. Hartford, Connecticut: Yale University Press, 1979.

Bullard, Major General Robert Lee. *Personalities and Reminiscences of the War*. New York: Doubleday, Page and Company, 1925.

Calendar of Historical Manuscripts Relating to the War of the Revolution, Vol. I. n.p: Albany, NY, 1868.

Carter, Allene G. and Robert L. Allen. *Honoring Sergeant Carter: Redeeming a Black World War II Hero's Legacy*. New York: Amistad, An Imprint of Harper Collins Publishers, 2003.

Cayton, Horace R. and St. Clair Drake. *Black Metropolis*. London: Jonathan Cape, 1946.

Clark, Byron N. (ed.). *A List of Pensioners of the War of 1812: With an Appendix containing names of Volunteers for the defense of Plattsburgh from Vermont towns*. Burlington, Vermont: n.p. 1904, reprinted Baltimore, Genealogical Pub. Co., 1969.

Clarke, William P. Major. *Official History of the Militia and National Guard of the State of Pennsylvania*, Vol. III. n.p., 1912.

Columbia County in the World War. The Home Defense Committee of Columbia County, New York. Albany: J.B. Lyon Company, 1924.

The Colonial Laws of New York, 1664 to the Revolution. Vol. V. Albany, NY: n.p., 1894–1896.

Cook, William R. and Eric C. Huynh. *Around Dansville*. Charleston, SC: Arcadia Publishing, 2006.

Cornish, Dudley T. *The Sable Arm: Negro Troops in The Union Army, 1861–1865*. New York: W.W. Norton and Company, Incorporated, NY, 1966.

Crow, Jeffrey. *The Black Experience in Revolutionary North Carolina*. Raleigh: Division North Carolina Archives and History, 1977.

Cruikshank, E. *Butler's Rangers: The Revolutionary Period*. Lundy's Lane Historical Society, 1893.

Cunliffe, Marcus. *Soldiers and Civilians*. Boston: Little, Brown and Co., 1968.

Davis, Barbara Sheklin. *Syracuse African Americans*. Charleston, SC: Arcadia Publishing, 2005.

DeCastelbled, Maurice. *History of the A.E.F., compiled from the records of the War Department Order of Battle of the United States Land Forces in the World War and from the Final Report of General John J. Pershing*. New York, Bookcraft, 1937.

DeLancey, Edward F. (ed.). *Muster Rolls of New York Provincial Troops, 1755–1764*. New York 1891, reprinted Bowie, Maryland: Heritage Books, 1990.

Dodson, Howard, Christopher Moore, and Roberta Yancy. *The Black New Yorkers: The Schomburg Illustrated Chronology*. New York: John Wiley and Sons, Inc., 2000.

Doubler, Michael D. and John W. Listman Jr. *The National Guard: An Illustrated History of America's Citizen Soldiers*. Washington: Brassey's Inc., 2003.

Drothing, Philip T. *Black Heroes in Our Nation's History*. New York: Washington Square Press, 2nd printing, 1971.

DuBois, W.E.B. *The Suppression of the African Slave-Trade to the United States of America 1638–1870*. n. p. 1896, New York: Schocken Edition, 1969.

Edward, Lieutenant F.E. *The '98 Campaign of the 6th Massachusetts U.S.V.* Boston: Little, Brown and Company, 1899.

Eisenstadt, Peter, Editor in Chief. *The Encyclopedia of New York*. Syracuse University Press, 2005.

Ellis, David; James A Frost; Harold Syrett; Harry F Carman. *A Short History of New York State*. Ithaca, NY: New York Historical Association, Cornell University Press, Third Printing, 1962.

Elting, John R. (ed.). *Military Uniforms in America: Long Endure: The Civil War Period, 1852–1867, from the Series Produced by the Company of Military Historians*. Novato, California: Presidio Press, 1982.

Elting, John R. and Mike McAfee, (ed). *Military Uniforms in America: The Modern Era from 1868, Volume IV, from the Series Produced by the Company of Military Historians*. California: Presidio Press, 1988.

Emerson, George D. *The Perry's Victory Centenary*. Albany: J.B. Lyon Company Publisher, 1916.

Emilio, Luis F. *A Brave Black Regiment: History of the Fifty-Fourth Regiment of Massachusetts Volunteer Infantry, 1863–1865*. Boston: The Boston Book Company, 1894, reprinted New York: Arno Press and the New York Times, 1969.

Evans, Captain Stephen H., U.S.C.G. *The United States Coast Guard, 1790–1915, A Definitive History*. Annapolis, Maryland: United States Naval Institute, 1949.

Fletcher, Marvin E. *America's First Black General, Benjamin O. Davis Sr., 1880–1970*. Lawrence, Kansas: University of Kansas, 1989.

Foner, Jack D. *Blacks and the Military in American History: a New Perspective*. New York and Washington: Praeger Publishers, 1974.

Forty, George. *US Marine Corps Handbook, 1941–1945*. United Kingdom: Sutton Publishing Limited, 2006.

Fowler, Arlen L. *The Black Infantry in the West, 1869–1891*. Westport, Connecticut: A Negro University Press Publication, Greenwood Publishing Corporation, 1972.

Fox, William F. Lt. Col., U.S.V. *Regimental Losses in the American Civil War, 1861–1865*. Albany, NY: Albany Publishing Company, 1893.

Francis, Charles E. (1st Lt. USAF-Res.). *The Tuskegee Airman: The Story of the Negro in the U.S. Air Force*. Boston: Brice Humphries, Inc., Publisher, 1955.

Franklin, John Hope. *From Slavery to Freedom: A History of Negro Americans*. New York: Alfred A. Knopf, Inc., 1947 and 1956.

———. *Mirror to America: The Autobiography of John Hope Franklin*. New York: Farrar, Straus and Giroux, 2005.

Gatewood, William B. *Smoked Yankees and the Struggle for Empire: Letters from Negro Soldiers, 1898–1902*. Chicago: University of Illinois Press, 1971.

Gero, Anthony and Roger Sturcke. *Cayugans in the Field-1793–2003: Citizen Soldiers of Cayuga County, New York*. Auburn: Jacobs Press, 2004.

———. *New York State National Guard*. Charleston, SC: Arcadia Publishing, 2006.

Gibb, C.R. *Black, Copper & Bright (The District of Columbia's Black Civil War Regiment)*. Silver Springs, Maryland: Three Dimensional Publishing, 2002.

Gladstone, William A. *United States Colored Troops, 1863–1867*. Gettysburg, Pennsylvania: Thomas Publication, 1990.

Glatthaar, Joseph T. *Forged in Battle: The Civil War Alliance of Black Soldiers and White Officers*. New York: The Free Press, a Division of Macmillian Inc., 1990.

Greene, Robert E. *Black Defenders of America, 1775–1973*. Chicago: Johnson Pub. Co. Inc., 1974.

Half-Shire Historical Society. *Northern Oswego County*. Charleston, SC: Arcadia Publishing, 2003.

Hall, Charles W. (ed.). *Regiments and Armories of Massachusetts*. Boston: W.W. Porter Company, 1899.

Hall, Gwendolyn Midlo (ed.). *Love, War, the 96th Engineers (Colored)*. Urbana: University of Illinois Press, 1995.

Hartzell, Karl D. (PhD). *The Empire State at War: World War II, Compiled and Written for the New York State War Council*. Albany: Published by the State of New York, 1949.

Hasting, Hugh (State Historian of New York). *Military Minutes of the Council of Appointments of the State of New York, 1783–1821*. Albany: J.B. Lyon, State Printer, 1902.

Hasting, Hugh (State Historian). *Public Papers of Daniel D. Tompkins, Governor of New York, 1807–1817*, Volume I. New York and Albany: Wynkoop Hallenbeck Crawford Company, State Printers, 1898 and Volume III, Albany: B. Lyon Company, State Printer, 1903.

Hazen, Margaret Hindle and Robert M Hazen. *The Music Men: An Illustrated History of Brass Bands in America, 1800–1920*. Washington, DC: Smithsonian Institution, 1987.

Heitman, Francis B. *Historical Register and Dictionary of the United States Army, Volume I*. Washington, DC, Government Printing Office, 1903.

Henri, Florette. *Bitter Victory, A History of Black Soldiers in World War I*. Garden City, New York: Zenith Books, 1979.

Higgins, Mary T. *Thomas Wentworth Higginson: The Story of His Life*. Boston and New York: Houghton and Mifflin and Company, 1914.

Hill, Jim Dan. *The Minute Man in Peace and War: A History of the National Guard*. Harrisburg, Pennsylvania: The Stackpole Company, 1964.

Historical Annual: National Guard and Naval Militia of the State of Ohio. Baton Rouge, Army and Navy Publishing Company, 1938.

Holmes, Jack D.L. *Honor and Fidelity: The Louisiana Infantry Regiment and the Louisiana Militia Companies, 1766–1821.* Birmingham: Louisiana Collection Series of Books and Documents on Colonial Louisiana, 1965.

Hunton, Addie W. and Kathryn M. Johnson. *Two Colored Women With the American Expeditionary Force.* Brooklyn: Brooklyn Eagle Press, 1920.

Jantzen, Steven. *Hooray for Peace, Hurrah for War, The United States During World War I.* New York and Scarborough, Ontario: Times Mirror, 1971.

Johnson, Jesse J. (Lt-Col., AUS-Ret.), ed. *The Black Soldier (Documented), 1619–1815: Missing Pages in United States History.* Hampton, Virginia: Hampton Institute, 1969.

Johnson, Charles Jr. *African American Soldiers in the National Guard.* Westport, Connecticut: Greenwood Press, 1992.

Katz, William Loren. *Eyewitness: The Negro in American History.* New York: Pitman Publishing Corporation, 1969.

Kennedy, David M. *Over Here: The First World War and American Society.* New York: Oxford University Press, 1980.

Knight, Erastus (Comptroller) and Frederic G. Mather. (ed). *New York in the Revolution as Colony and State: Supplement.* Albany, New York: Oliver A. Quayle, 1901.

Kreidberg, Marvin A. (Lt-Col.) and G. Henry Merton (1st Lt.). *History of Military Mobilization in the United States Army, 1775–1945.* Washington, DC: Department of the Army, 1955.

Krutz, David P. *Distant Drums: Herkimer County in the War of the Rebellion.* Utica: New York, North Country Books, 1997.

Lanard, Thomas S. *One Hundred Years with the State Fencibles: a History of the Infantry Corps, Infantry Battalion and Old Guard State Fencibles, 1813–1913.* Philadelphia: Nields Co., 1913.

Lanctot, Neil. *Fair Dealings and Clean Playing: The Hillsdale Club and the Development of Black Professional Baseball, 1910–1932.* Jefferson, N. Carolina: McFarland and Company, Inc., 1994.

Lanning, Michael Lee, Lt-Col. (Ret.). *The African-American Soldier: from Crispus Attucks to Colin Powell.* Secaucus, New Jersey: A Citadel Press Book, 1997.

Lechie, William H. *The Buffalo Soldiers: A Narrative of the Negro Cavalry in the West*. Norman: University of Oklahoma Press, 1967.

Lee, Irvin H. *Negro Medal of Honor Men*. New York: Dodd, Meade and Company, 1967.

Lee, Ulysses. *United States Army in World War 2: Special Studies: The Employment of Negro Troops*. Washington, DC: Office of the Chief of Military History, U.S. Army, 1966.

Lefferts, Charles M. (Lt.). *Uniforms of the American, British, French and German Armies in the War of the American Revolution*, 1926, reprinted by Old Greenwich, Connecticut, We. Inc.

Little, Arthur W. *From Harlem to the Rhine: The Story of New York's Colored Volunteers*. New York: Corvice and Friede Publishing, 1936.

Logan, Rayford W. *The Betrayal of the Negro from Rutherford B. Hayes to Woodrow Wilson*. New York: Collier Books, New Enlarged Edition, 1965.

Mabee, Carlto. *Black Education in New York State: From Colonial to Modern Times*. Syracuse, New York: Syracuse University Press, 1979.

Madison County's Welcome Home. Oneida, New York: The Oneida Dispatch Press, 1919.

Mahon, John K. *The War of 1812*. Gainesville: University of Florida Press, 1972.

Mahon, John K. *History of the Second Seminole War, 1835–1842*. Gainesville, Florida: University of Florida Press, 1967.

Marszalek, John F. *Court Martial: The Army Vs Johnson Whittaker: An Account of the Ordeal of a Black Cadet at West Point in 1881*. New York: Charles Scribner's Sons, 1972.

Matthews, Harry Bradshaw. *Honoring New York's Forgotten Soldiers: African Americans of the Civil War*. Oneonta, New York: n.p., 1998.

Maynard, Joan and Gwen Cottman. *Weeksville, Then and Now*. Brooklyn, New York: The Society for the Preservation of Weeksville and Bedford-Stuyvesant History, 1983.

McAlexander, Captain U. G. *History of the 13th Regiment United States Infantry*. n.p., 1905.

McConnell, Roland. *Negro Troops of Antebellum Louisiana: A History of the Battalion of Free Men of Color*. Baton Rouge: Louisiana State University Press, 1968.

McKay, Ernest A. *The Civil War and New York City*. Syracuse, New York: Syracuse University Press, 1990.

McMaster, Fitzhugh. *Soldiers and Uniforms: South Carolina Military Affairs, 1670–1775*. Columbia, Tricentennial Booklet Number 10, University of South Carolina Press, 1971.

McPherson, James M. *The Negroes Civil War: How American Negroes Felt And Acted During The War For The Union*. New York: Vintage Books, a Division of Random House, 1965.

Mead, Gary. *The Doughboys: America and the First World War*. Woodstock and New York: The Overlook Press, 2000.

Morris, Robert V. *Tradition and Valor: a Family Journey*. Manhattan, Kansas: Sunflower University Press, 1999.

Muller, William G., then Capt. and Adjutant. *The Twenty Fourth Infantry, Past and Present*. Ft. Collins, Colorado: reprinted by the Old Army Press, 1972.

Nankivell, Henry H., Major. *History of the Military Organization of the State of Colorado, 1860–1935*. n.p.: printed in 1935.

Nell, William C. *The Colored Patriots of the American Revolution*. Boston: R. F. Wallicut, 1855.

Nelson, Brig. General Harold W. (USA-Ret.), Editor in Chief; Major Gen. Bruce Jacobs (AUS-Ret.), Editor; Colonel Raymond Bluhm Jr., (USA-Ret.); Graphics Editor. *The Army*. Arlington, Virginia: The Army Historical Foundation, Beaux Arts Edition, 2001.

Nevins, Allan and Halsey Thomas Milton (ed.). *The Diary of George Templeton Strong: The Civil War, 1860–1866*. New York: The Macmillian Company, 1952.

Nye, Wilbur Sturtevant. *Here Come The Rebels*. Louisiana State Press, 1965, reprinted by Morningside House Inc., 1988.

Pargellis, Stanley. *Military Affairs in North America, 1748–1765*. New York, 1936.

Patton, Gerald W. *War and Race: The Black Officer in the American Military, 1915–1941*. Westport, Connecticut: Greenwood Press, 1981.

Pershing, John J. *My Experience in the World War, Volumes 1 and 2*. New York: Frederick A. Stokes Comp., 1931.

Phisterer, Frederick. *New York in the War of the Rebellion, 1861–1865.* Albany: L.B. Lyon Company, State Printer, Volume I, 1912.

Potter, Lou with William Miles, and Nina Rosenblum. *Liberators: Fighting on Two Fronts in World War II.* New York: Harcourt Brace Jovanovich, 1992.

Quarles, Benjamin. *The Negro in the American Revolution.* Chapel Hill: Published for the Institute of Early American History and Culture at Williamsburg, Virginia by the University of North Carolina Press, 1961.

Rampersad, Arnold. *Jackie Robinson: a biography.* New York: Alfred A. Knopf, 1997.

Redkey, Edwin S. *A Grand Army of Black Men: Letters from African-American Soldiers in the Union Army, 1861–1865.* New York: Cambridge University Press, 1992.

Reed, George A. and Carole Reed. *Images of America: Fort Ontario: Guardian of the North.* Charleston, South Carolina: Arcadia Publishing, 2000.

Richards, Brig. Genl. J.J. *Rhode Island's Early Defenders and the Successors.* n.p., 1937.

Richter, William L. *The Army in Texas During Reconstruction, 1865–1870.* College Station: Texas A&M University Press, 1987.

Robinson, Wilhemina S. *Historical Negro Biographies, under the auspices of the Association for the Study of Negro Life and History.* New York: Publisher Company, Incorporated, 1967.

Romero, Patricia W. (ed.). *International Library of Afro-American Life and History, I Too Am American: Documents from 1619 to the Present, Volume I.* The Association for the Study of Afro-American Life and History, 1978.

Saunders, Ernest. *Blacks in the Connecticut National Guard, A pictorial and chronological history, 1870–1919.* New Haven: New Haven Afro-American Historical Society, Inc., 1977.

Sawicki, James A. *Infantry Regiments of the U.S. Army.* Dumfries, Virginia: Wyvern Publications, 1981.

Scott, Emmett. *Scott's Official History of the American Negro in the World War.* n.p., 1919.

Seymour, Harold. *Baseball: The People's Game*. New York: Oxford University Press, 1990.

Shaw, Henry I., and Ralph W Donnelly. *Blacks in the Marine Corps*. Washington, DC: History and Museum Division, Headquarters, USMC, 1975.

Simmons, William J. *Men of Mark: Eminent, Progressive and Rising*. Geo. M. Rewell & Co., 1887, reprinted by the Johnson Company, Inc., 1970.

Singletary, Otis. *Negro Militia and Reconstruction*. Texas: University of Texas Press, 1957.

Smythe, Donald. *Guerrilla Warrior, The Early Life of John J. Pershing*. New York, 1973.

Stallings, Laurence. *The Doughboys: The Story of the A.E.F., 1917–1918*. New York: Harper and Row, 1963.

Stanton, Shelby L. (Capt. USA-Ret.). *World War II: Order of Battle*. New York: Galahad Books, 1984.

Sterling, Dorothy (ed.). *The Trouble They Seen: The Story of Reconstruction in the Words of African Americans*. New York: De Capo Press, 1994.

Strick, Lisa W. *The Black Presence in the Era of the American Revolution, 1770–1800*. Washington, DC: Smithsonian Institution, 1973.

Sweeney, W. Allison. *History of the American Negro in the Great World War*. Chicago: 1919.

Swift-Hoyt, Hildegarde. *The Railroad to Freedom: A Story of the Civil War*. New York: Harcourt, Brace and Company, 1932.

Todd, Colonel Frederick P. *American Military Equipage, 1851–1872: Volume II: State Forces*. USA: Chatham Square Press, Inc., 1983.

Todd, Colonel Frederick P., and Major Kenneth C. Miller. *Pro Patria et Gloria: the illustrated story of the hundred and fifty years of the Seventh Regiment of New York*. Hartsdale, New York: Rampart House, 1956.

Todd, Nancy L. *New York's Historic Armories: An Illustrated History*. Albany: State University of New York Press, 2006.

Todish, Timothy J. and Gary S. Zaboly. *The Annotated and Illustrated Journals of Major Robert Rogers*. Fleischmanns, New York: Purple Mountain Press, LTD., 2002.

Trudeau, Noah Andre. *Like Men of War: Black Troops in the Civil War 1862–1865.* Edison, New Jersey: Castle Books, 2002.

Wellman, Judith, Project Coordinator. *Uncovering the Freedom Trail in Auburn and Cayuga County, New York: A Cultural Resource Survey.* Fulton, New York, FTS Inc., 2005.

White, David O. *Connecticut's Black Soldiers, 1775–1783.* Connecticut: the Pequot Press, 1973.

Wilkes, Laura. *Missing Pages in American History: Revealing The Services Of Negroes In the Early Wars In The United States of America, 1641–1815.* Washington, DC: Press of R.L. Pendelton, 1919.

Williams-Myers, A.J. *Long Hammering: Essays on the Forging of an African American Presence in the Hudson River Valley to the Early Twentieth Century.* Trenton, New Jersey: Africa World Press, Inc., 1994.

Wilson, Joseph T. *The Black Phalanx.* Hartford: American Publishing Co., 1889.

Winks, Robin. *The Blacks in Canada: a History.* New Haven and London: McGill-Queen University Press, Montreal, but published by Yale University Press, 1971.

Wisnoski, Donald M. *The Opportunity is at Hand: Oneida County, New York, Colored Soldiers in the Civil War.* Lynchburg, Virginia: Schroeder Publications, 2003.

Woodson, Carter G., PhD. *The Negro In Our History.* Washington, DC: The Associated Publishers, Inc., 7th Edition, 1941.

Wright, Kai. *Soldiers of Freedom: An Illustrated History of African Americans in the Armed Forces.* New York: Black Dog & Leventhal, 2002.

Wright, Robert K. *Army Lineage Series: The Continental Army.* Washington, DC: Center of Military History, United States Army, 1983.

Yellin, Jean Fagan. *Harriet Jacobs: A Life.* Basic Civitas Books, a member of the Perseus Books Group, 2004.

Articles

Abbott, David C. and Anthony Gero. "Company L, 6th Massachusetts Volunteer Infantry, 1898–1899, (plate No. 467)." *Military Collector and Historian,* Vol. XXX, No. 4, Winter 1978.

Aptheker, Herbert. "The Negro in the Union Navy." *Journal of Negro History*, Vol. XXXII, April 1947.

Archambault, Alan and Marko Zlatich. "Rhode Island Regiment, 1781–1783, plate No. 559." *Military Uniforms in America*, as published by the Company of Military Historians, Rutland, MA, 1984.

Archambault, Alan and Anthony Gero. "United States Colored Troops, Enlisted Men, Infantry, 1864–1865, Plate No. 736." *Military Uniforms in America*, as published by the Company of Military Historians, Rutland, MA, 1996.

Cole, Merle T., Captain MDSG. "Maryland's State Defense Force." *Military Collector and Historian*, Vol. XXXIX, No. 4, Winter 1987.

Cunningham, Roger. "The Virginia Militia at the National Drill, 1887." *Virginia Cavalcade*, Volume 49, Number 4, Autumn 2000.

————. "Missouri's Black Immunes in the Spanish-American War." *Military Collector and Historian*, Washington, DC, Volume 56, No. 1, 2004.

Copeland, Peter F. and James P. Simpson. "11th New Hampshire Provincial Regiment, 1774–1775." *Military Uniforms in America: The Era of the American Revolution, 1755–1795*, the Company of Military Historians, edited by John R. Elting, Presidio Press, 1974.

Cummings, James J. "The Black 369th in Oswego(1941)." *Journal 1972*, Oswego County Historical Society, 1973.

Curtis, John. O. "Jack Lee of Rowley, Massachusetts: A Black New Englander in the Nineteenth Century Massachusetts Militia." *Military Collector and Historian*, Vol. 54. No. 2, Summer 2002.

Falls, Colonel DeWitt Clinton. "369th Infantry." *New York Guardsman Magazine*, October 1928.

Gero, Anthony. "Some Notes on New York's Black Regiments." *Military Collector and Historian*, Vol. XXXI, No. 1, Spring 1979.

————. "The use of Ex-Slaves in the Royal Marines, circa 1814–1815." *Military Collector and Historian*, Vol. XXXI, No. 4, Winter 1979.

————. "Jordan B. Noble, Black drummer of the Seventh Regiment, U.S. Infantry, 1813–1815." *Military Collector and Historian*, Vol. XXXI, No. 1, Spring 1979.

————. "American Deserter Notices in the Northern Theater, 1813 to 1815." *Military Collector and Historian,* Vol. XXXVIII, No. 2, Summer 1986.

————. "A Report of New York Afro-Americans in the War of 1812: August 1814." *Military Collector and Historian,* Vol. XLIV, No. 3, Fall 1992.

————. and Philip G. Maples. "Notes on the Dress of the 13th Regiment, United States Infantry, 1812–1813." *Military Collector and Historian*, Vol. XLV, No. 4, Winter 1993.

————. "The Cornell Cadet Corps, 1869–1929." *Military Collector and Historian*, Vol. 53, No. 1, Spring 2001.

————. "Observations on the Infantry Uniform of the New York State Militia, 1820–1835." *Military Collector and Historian*, Vol. XXXVI, No 4, Winter 1984.

————. and Philip G. Maples. "Fusileering in Western New York, 1830–1840." *Military Collector and Historian*, Vol. XXXII, No. 3, Fall 1980.

————. and Philip G. Maples. "5th Battalion (Colored), Connecticut National Guard, circa, 1879."*Military Collector and Historian*, Vol. XXXVI, No. 2, Summer, 1984.

————. "Independent Afro-American Military Companies, 1854–1860: Some Observations." *Military Collector and Historian*, Vol. XLVI, No. 1, Spring 1992.

————. with Richard Warren, and Roger Sturcke. "54th Regiment, Massachusetts Volunteer Infantry, 1863–1865, Plate No. 556" in *Military Uniforms in America*, published by the Company of Military Historians, Rutland, MA.

————. "The Onondaga Colored Battalion, 1876–1877." *Military Collector and Historian*, Vol. XXXIV, No. 3, Fall 1982.

————. with Raymond Johnson. "A Brief Sketch of the Afro-American Combat Volunteers, 104th Infantry Division, 1945." *Military Collector and Historian*, Vol. XLVIII, No. 3, Fall 1996.

Gordon, Martin K. "The Black Militia in the District of Columbia." *Records* of the Columbia Historical Society of Washington, DC, 1971–1972, Published by the Society, Distributed by the University of Virginia, 1973.

Hartgrove, W.B. "The Negro Soldier in the American Revolution." *Journal of Negro History*, Vol. 1, No. 2, April 1916.

Hirsch, Leo H., Jr. "The Negro and New York, 1783–1865." *Journal of Negro History*, Vol. XVI, 1931.

Johnson, Raymond and Rick Ugino. "21st Regiment, New York Guard, 1940–1945." MUIA plate 548, *Military Collector and Historian*, Vol. XXXV, No. 4, Winter 1983.

Johnson, Raymond and Anthony Gero. "78th Division Field Uniforms, 1943–1945." *Military Collector and Historian*, Vol. XXXIX, No. 2, Summer 1987.

Kolakowski, Christopher L. "A Sister's Journey to the Western Front in 1920."*Military Collector and Historian*, Vol. 56, No. 3, Fall 2004.

Logan, Raymond. "The Negro in the Quasi War, 1798–1800." *The Negro History Bulletin*, March 1951.

Long, Howard, M. "The Negro Soldier in the Army of the United States." *Journal of Negro Education*, Vol. 12, Summer 1943.

McBarron, H. Charles Jr., and Frederick P. Todd and John R. Elting. "Chatham Light Dragoons, Georgia Volunteer Militia, 1811–1816." *MUIA: Years of Growth, 1796–1851*, edited by John R. Elting, from the Series Produced by the Company of Military Historians, Presidio Press, 1977.

McBarron, H. Charles, Jr. and Detmar Finke. "U.S. Corps of Artificers, 1812–1815." *MUIA: Years of Growth, 1796–1851*, edited by John R. Elting, from the Series Produced by the Company of Military Historians, Presidio Press, 1977.

Military Images. "African-Americans In the Great War: 1917–1919." Volume XXVII, Number 4, Jan/Feb., 2006.

Northrup, A. Judd. "Slavery in New York." *State Library Bulletin, History*, No. 4, May 1900, University of the State of New York, Albany, 1900.

Rapp, Scott. "Slain Soldier Honored: Man was Cayuga County's only black soldier killed in World War II." *The Post-Standard*, November 18, 2004.

Rodgers, Thomas G. "Georgia's Volunteer Militia, 1872–1898." *Military Collector and Historian*, Vol. 59, No. 2, Summer 2007.

Seraile, William. "The Struggle to Raise Black Regiments in New York State, 1861–1864." *The New York Historical Society Quarterly*, Volume LVIII, July 1974, No. 3.

Sheads, Scott S. "A Black Soldier Defends Fort McHenry." *Military Collector and Historian*, Vol. XLI, No. 1, Spring 1989.

Thompson, Barry and Orton Begner, and Anthony Gero. "371st Infantry Regiment, 93rd Division, 1917–1919, Plate No. 488." *Military Collector and Historian*, Vol. XXXI, No. 3, Fall 1979.

Till, Paul H. "NYNG and NYG Insignia, Part V." *Trading Post*, October–December, 1985.

Zaboly, Gary and John R. Elting. "3rd New York Battalion, 1758, Plate No. 541." *Military Collector and Historian*, Vol. XXXI, No. 2, Summer 1983.

Zaboly, Gary S. "Occupied New York Extracts on the Uniforms, Arms, and Equipment of the British Army and Navy from Royalist Newspapers, 1776–1783." *Military Collector and Historian*, Vol. 56, No. 3, Fall 2004.

Internet

The New York State Military Museum and Veterans Research Center at: http://www.dmna.state.n.y.us

Historic Weeksville: weeksvillesociety.org

"Old Fulton NY Post Cards:" http://www.fultonhistory.com/Fulton.html

Newspapers/Magazine

Auburn Daily Advertiser and Union (Auburn, New York), 1863

Citizen-Advertiser (Auburn, New York), 1942

Harpers Weekly, 1864

New York Daily Tribune, 1864–1865

New York Herald, 1814

The Citizen-Advertiser (Auburn, New York), 1935

The Citizen-Advertiser (Auburn, New York), 1945

The Independent and Harpers' Weekly, 1919

The New York Times, 1871

The New York Times, 1876

The New York Times, 1916–1918

The New York Times, 1942–1949
The Oswego Palladium Times (Oswego), 1941
The Post-Standard (Syracuse, New York), 2004
The Post-Standard (Syracuse, New York), 2007
The Syracuse Courier (Syracuse, New York), 1880
The Syracuse Journal (Syracuse, New York), 1880

Suggestions for Further Research

The Afro-American Historical and Genealogical Society's Web site: www. AAHGS.org.

Barrow, Charles and J.H. Segars, R.B. Rosenburg (eds.). *Forgotten Confederates: An Anthology About Black Southerners*. Journal of Confederate History Series, Vol. XIV. Atlanta, Georgia: Southern Heritage Press, 1995.

Groene, Bertram Hawthorne. *Tracing Your Civil War Ancestor, a complete guide to tracking down your ancestor's Civil War adventures, North and South*. New York Ballatine Books, 1973.

Hewen, Janet B. (ed.) *The Roster of Union Soldiers, 1861–1865: United States Colored Troops, M589-1-M589*. Wilmington, North Carolina: Broadfoot Publishing Company, 1991.

Hoff, Henry B. "Researching African-American Families in New Netherland and Colonial New York and New Jersey." *The New York Genealogical and Biographical Record*, Volume 136, Number 2, April 2005.

Johnson, Richard, Lt. Col. and Debra Johnson Knox. *How to Locate Anyone Who Is or Has Been in the Military: Armed Forces Locator Guide, Eight Edition*. Spartanburg, SC: Military Information Enterprize, Inc., 1999.

Kelbaugh, Ross J. *Introduction to African American Photographs, 1840–1950, Identification, Research, Care & Collecting*. Gettysburg, Pennsylvania: Thomas Publications, 2005.

Murray, Pauli. *Proud Shoes: The Story of an American Family*. New York: Harper and Row, 1956, revised 1978.

Thomas, William G. and Alice E. Carter. *The Civil War on the Web, A Guide to the Very Best Sites*. Wilmington, Delaware: A Scholarly Resource Inc. Imprint, 2001.

United States Colored Troops Institute for Local History and Family Research: Hartwick College, Oneonta, New York, 13820: Web site at: http://www.hartwick.edu/usct.

Index

Addison, Joseph, quoted, xii

African-American women in the Civil War, 26

Alabama
  black volunteers in Spanish-American War, 36
  blacks in militia before the Spanish-American War, 32

Albany, New York, possible recruitment center for 54th Massachusetts Volunteer Infantry, 25

American Expeditionary Force (AEF) in World War I. *See* United States Army

Andrews, Governor John (Massachusetts)
  appoints black line officers in the Civil War, 25
  attitudes toward black volunteers in the Civil War, 24

Appleton, Major Charles L., 367th Infantry, cited for bravery in World War I, 59

Attucks Guards of Cincinnati, Ohio, 1855, 20

Attucks Guards of New York City, 1855, 19, 21

Auburn, New York
  African-Americans in World War I, 60–61
  African-Americans in World War II, 89–91
  black volunteers in the Civil War, 23, 25
  Harriet Tubman's service in the Civil War, 25
  home of William H. Seward, 25

Bakeman, Henry, in Colonel Marinus Willet's 1783 campaign against Oswego, New York, 8

Baker, Secretary of War Newton D., attitudes toward African-Americans, 42, 46–47, 69

Ballou, General Charles C., former commander of 92nd

Bullard, Eugene Jacques, volunteers for French Foreign Legion in World War I, 40

Bullard, General Robert L., former commander 2nd American Army, AEF, views against black soldiers, 69

Burnell, Marsden V. (New York City), barred from CMTC training, 72

Butler's Rangers, British Loyalist unit has African-Americans serving in, 8

California
colored company in its national guard in 1870s, 32
369th CA (AA) sent to Camp Stoneman in 1942, 81

Camps
Camp Alger (Virginia) in 1898, 37
Camp Dix (New Jersey) racial incident in 1919, 62
Camp Edwards (Massachusetts) in World War II, 81
Camp Meade (Maryland) in 1919, 60
Camp Smith (New York) in World War II, 83–84
Camp Steward (Georgia) in World War II, 81
Camp Stoneman (California) in World War II, 81
Camp Upton (New York) during 1917–1919, 58, 60, 63

Canada
black soldiers who fought on the British side in Revolution settle there after the war, 8

black volunteers serve in 54th Massachusetts Volunteer Infantry in the Civil War, 25

Canadian Voltigeurs in War of 1812, possible service of black men in, 15

Captain Robert Runchey's Company of Black Men in the War of 1812, 14–15

Capital Guards of Denver, Colorado in the 1880s, 32

Carter, Elmer, service in 325th Signal Battalion, 92nd Division in World War I, 61. See also Auburn, New York

Cayuga County, New York
African-American soldiers during the Civil War, 23, 25, 27
black soldiers' participation in World War I, 60–61
black soldiers' participation in World War II, 89–91
Harriet Tubman service in the military during the Civil War, 25
Underground Rail Road in Cayuga County, 61, 125n75

Cayuga Museum of History and Art, Auburn, New York, 26–27, 91

Cazenovia, New York, integrated Grand Army of the Republic Post, 26

Central Committee of Negro College Men meets with President Wilson, 42

Noble, Jordan B., mulatto
drummer in 7th Regiment
United States Infantry in
War of 1812, 13, 15
Noil, Seaman Joseph B., earns
Medal of Honor in 1872, 31
North Carolina
black volunteers in 1898, 36
blacks in militia in the French
and Indian War, 3
nurses, African-American women
serve in World War I, 43,
120n7

Ohio
Attucks Guards, 1855, 20
black soldiers in the Ohio
National Guard prior in
1917, 32, 43
blacks in the militia in 1880s
and 1890s, 32
blacks in 1898 accepted as
volunteers, 32, 36
Wilberforce University,
African-American ROTC, 78
Oneida County, New York,
service of black volunteers in
the Civil War, 26
Onondaga Colored Battalion,
Syracuse, New York, in
1870s, 34–36
Orange County, New York,
African-Americans service in
county's colonial militia, 2
Orangetown, New York, 5
Oswego, New York
African-American volunteers
enlist in the 54th Regiment
Massachusetts Volunteers, 25

British fort unsuccessfully
attacked there in 1783 by
Rhode Island Regiment, 8
24th USI, a segregated Regular
Army regiment, has elements
stationed at Fort Ontario, 38
369th CA (AA) stationed at
Fort Ontario in 1941, 81
Otsego County, New York,
service of black volunteers in
the Civil War, 26
Over There (song), 51

Paige, Major Myles A.,
commander of the 3rd
Separate Battalion, NYG in
World War II, 83–86
Palmer Guards, Onondaga
County, New York, possibly
an African-American military
unit, 35–36
Peekskill, New York
camp in 1917, 49
camp in 1920s and 1930s, 71
service of African-American
New York Guard units in
World War II, 83–86
Pennington, Reverend James W. C.
activities in the Civil War, 23
heads African-American
delegation in Lincoln's
funeral procession in 1865, 27
Pennsylvania
blacks in the militia in 1783–
1811, 9
in Gettysburg campaign of
1863, blacks form militia
units to help repel invasion,
110–111n18

DATE DUE
